THE COMPLETE
BOOK OF
GOLF
TECHNIQUES

WHITECAP BOOKS

CLB 3412
This edition published in 1995 by
Whitecap Books Ltd., 351 Lynn Avenue
North Vancouver, B.C., Canada V7J 2C4
© Eaglemoss Publications Ltd 1989, 1990, 1991, 1992
Printed in Hong Kong
ISBN 1-55110-361-3

PICTURE CREDITS

Front and back cover: Allsport; Phil Sheldon/Eaglemoss; Eaglemoss; Phil
Sheldon Photo Library; Colorsport; Dave Cannon (Allsport); Peter Dazeley.

Inside credits: 1 Yours in Sport; 2 Phil Sheldon Photo Library; 4(t) Allsport/
Dave Cannon; 4(b) Colorsport; 31 Allsport/Dave Cannon; 32 Phil Sheldon
Photo Library; 44 Charles Briscoe-Knight; 46 Phil Sheldon Photo Library;
48(b) Peter Dazley; 58 Allsport/Simon Bruty; 60(b) Golf Picture Library; 62
Allsport/Dave Cannon; 66 Phil Sheldon Photo Library; 68 Steve Carr; 70
Allsport/Dave Cannon; 90 Phil Sheldon Photo Library; 114(c) Brian Morgan;
128(b), 132(b), 134(r) Allsport/Dave Cannon; 138(b), 139, 140(b) Yours in
Sport; 140(l) Swilken Golf Company; 148(bl) Brian Morgan; 151, 158, 159
Charles Briscoe-Knight;170, 172(t) Golf Picture Library; 172(b), 174(t) Phil
Sheldon Photo Library; 174(b) Allsport/Dave Cannon; 175 Yours in Sport;
176(t) Peter Dazeley; 176(b) Allsport/Dave Cannon.

All other photographs: Phil Sheldon/Eaglemoss Publications.
All illustrations: Eaglemoss Publications.

·CONTENTS·

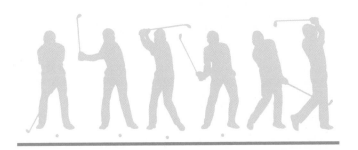

·INTRODUCTION·

There is something compelling about golf that makes you want to come back for more, whether you're playing well or suffering from a persistent problem. When your game is infuriatingly poor, it's a challenge; when you're scorching the fairways it's a drug – you want to play on and on. But whatever stage you are at – a relative beginner or a seasoned professional – there is always room for improvement. Not one of the world's finest players would ever claim to having completely mastered this game. Some have come close, but just around the corner there's a double bogey staring them in the face.

This book will help players of all levels to build up a sound knowledge of the golf swing as well as an understanding of the strategies that can make such a startling difference to a score.

Through concisely written instruction, telltale photographs and simple illustrations, golf becomes less of a puzzle. Have you ever wondered how to play a pitch and run, or a high lob over a bunker? Do you ever crave to be able to hit a draw off the tee or consistently hole those awkward six footers? Well, every detail is covered, and with practice and patience, the tips and drills will help you achieve your goals and make you a much more complete golfer.

Sam Snead demonstrates his distinctive putting style during the 1991 US Masters at Augusta.

Aim and grip

Before you can even think about hitting the ball you have to know where you want the ball to go and how to hold the club. Aim and grip are the first two of the fundamentals that must be correct or your shots will be off target. Even the most experienced golfer should constantly check that both his aim and grip are right. It is only too easy for a simple fault to creep into a good golfer's play at the most basic stage.

The concept behind aim applies to whatever type of stroke you are playing. You must have your clubface square to the ball-to-target line to hit the ball straight.

The grip described here is the standard grip – called the overlapping, or Vardon, grip – that you use on every club apart from the putter.

When you've mastered aim and grip you can then go on to think about alignment of your body and club, the ball position in relation to body position, and the posture needed to attain the correct swing. These pre-swing essentials are part of the pre-shot routine that gets you to the right address position – the position from which you can produce a good swing.

AIM THE CLUBFACE

Before you think about the grip, look at the ball and the target – whether it is the flagstick, or some point on the fairway – and imagine a line joining them. This is your ball-to-target line and is the line you want the ball to travel along. Look at your target two or three times to ensure that you see the line clearly in your mind's eye.

You aim the club simply by setting the leading edge of the clubface precisely at right angles to the line from your target to the ball. Rest the sole of the clubhead on the

ground behind the ball, hold the shaft in one hand and set the aim. It doesn't matter too much which club you use but a 6 or 7 iron is a good one to start off with. Stand so that your feet are about as far apart as your shoulders with your toes pointing outwards. The ball is about 1 ft (45cm) from the centre of your toe line.

When you go through the process of adjusting the grip, check every so often that the clubface is square to the ball-to-target line.

GRIP KNOW-HOW

The correct grip is vital and it is easy to adopt. It's important to remember that in the golf swing the hands play different roles and these roles are reflected in the way

ON TARGET
The correct aim and grip are essential if you want to hit the ball accurately and powerfully towards your target. At all times, while assuming the grip, the clubface should be square on to the imaginary line from the ball to the target.

TAKING UP THE OVERLAPPING GRIP

1 BEFORE YOU GRIP
Rest the clubhead on the ground and support the club with your right forefinger and thumb. Let your left arm hang naturally beside the club. Make sure the clubface is properly aimed.

2 THE LEFT HAND
Move your left hand on to the club and position the grip diagonally across the 'meat' of your hand. Close your third and little fingers – vital pressure points.

3 THUMB POSITION
Completely close your left hand, allowing your thumb to rest to the right of centre. Make sure your grip is not too tight.

TAKING AIM

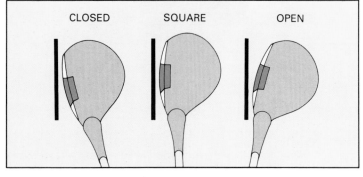

CLOSED   SQUARE   OPEN

The clubhead
Place the clubhead squarely behind the ball. If the clubface is open or closed, the flight of the golf ball is affected. Be extra careful when taking your grip not to alter the angle of the clubface.

they are used in the grip. The hands are placed in different positions and work together during the swing.

Your left hand supports the club and maintains the clubhead in the correct position through impact with the ball. It can be described as the 'strong hand' in the grip. The club is positioned diagonally across the palm, resting against the 'meat' of your hand.

Your right hand, however, is going to 'release' the club-head just before impact. This release gives the clubhead the power and speed to get maximum distance.

Releasing the clubhead is similar to the action of throwing a golf ball or skimming stones across water. When you do this you instinctively hold the stone somewhere between the forefinger and middle finger, with the thumb resting lightly on it as a support.

The release comes from the 'trigger finger' or, to be more precise, the middle joint of your forefinger.

When you hold the club with your right hand the grip should run through these fingers. By holding it this way you can be sure of a good release of power at the correct time.

When taking your grip, start by placing the sole of the club on the

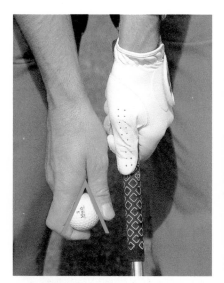

4 FORMING THE 'V'
Create the 'V', between thumb and forefinger, by holding a golf ball between the forefinger, middle finger and thumb of your right hand. Drop the ball by slightly releasing the pressure but keep your hand in the same position.

pro tip

Not so tight a squeeze

There's a simple way to get your grip pressure correct. Take a large tube of toothpaste and unscrew the cap. Hold the tube with the nozzle pointing down and grip the tube as you would your club. The pressure you exert should be just hard enough to hold the tube securely without squeezing the toothpaste out.

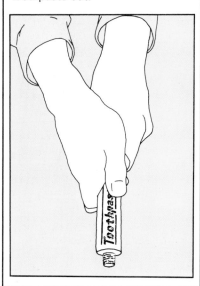

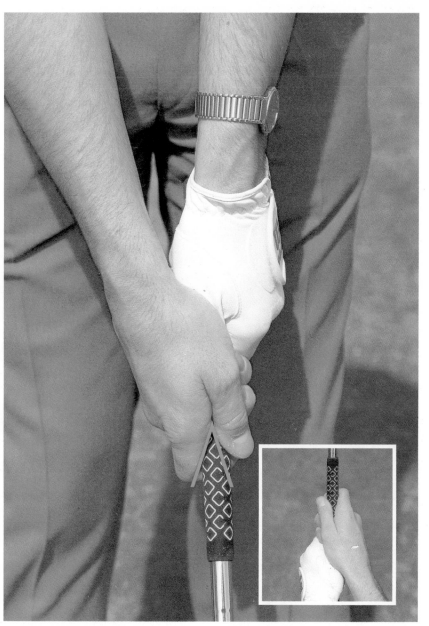

5 THE RIGHT HAND
Move your right hand on to the grip and hold the club with your two middle fingers and forefinger. Let your little finger overlap with the forefinger of your left hand and your right thumb rest to the left of centre of the shaft. Raise the club up to eye level. You should see two knuckles showing on each hand and a 'V' made by the thumb and forefinger of your right hand.

ground – preferably up against the ball on a tee peg as this helps you keep the clubhead square. Support the club using the tip of your right forefinger and thumb placed on the top of the grip.

THE LEFT HAND

Let your left arm hang naturally by the side of the grip before bringing it across to the club to take hold. About -1in (1.5-2.5cm) of the grip protrudes above where it rests across your hand. Your thumb should fall slightly to the right of centre and your third and little fingers should grip hardest. These are important pressure points. The club must rest diagonally across your palm, in the 'meat' of your hand.

THE RIGHT HAND

When you have the club correctly positioned in your left hand let go with your right hand and let it hang naturally by your side. The grip formed by your right hand should take up the form of a 'V' between your thumb and forefinger.

To get an idea of how the 'V' should look, hold a golf ball as if you are about to throw it. Drop the ball by slightly relaxing your grip and, with the grip still in place, bring your hand across to the club.

Grip the club below your left hand with the middle two fingers and forefinger of your right hand. Let the little finger of your right hand overlap with the forefinger of your left hand. The thumb of yourright hand should rest lightly on the grip pointing down the shaft and slightly to the left of centre. Check that the clubface is square.

When you have both hands on the club, lift it up to chest height. Take a good look at your hands – you should see two knuckles on each of your hands and a very pronounced 'V' in your right hand, pointing towards your chin. The hands are now completely moulded into one unit.

Why one glove ?
Most golfers wear a glove on their left hand (right hand for left handers). This is because the left hand supports the club, maintaining correct clubhead position through impact, and the glove gives you a more secure hold with the stronger hand.

OVERLAPPING GRIP
In the finished grip, the little finger of your right hand is over the forefinger of your left hand. It is the standard grip (also called Vardon grip) for all shots except putts. It is the best grip for most golfers.

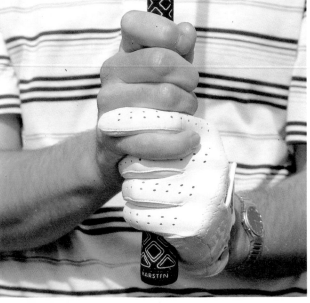

INTERLOCKING GRIP
If you have small hands or fingers try the interlocking grip. This is the same as the overlapping grip except that the little finger of your right hand interlocks with the forefinger of your left hand.

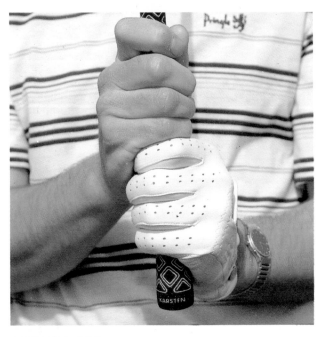

BASEBALL GRIP
This is an unusual grip in which all ten fingers are in contact with the grip. It is mainly used by players who are physically weak, such as youngsters and those suffering from arthritis.

pro tip

Leave a space
When taking your grip leave -1in (1.5-2.5cm) of the grip showing above your left hand. This secures your hold and prevents you straining the back two tendons of the left hand. It also prevents overswinging.

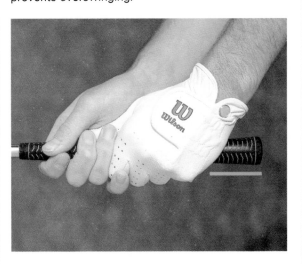

Posture and alignment

The right posture sets up your body in the correct position for the swing and proper alignment ensures that you hit the ball straight along the imaginary ball-to-target line.

Body position and alignment of the body are two of the five essentials necessary for a good swing, along with aim of the clubface, grip and ball placement. You need to know these basics and practise them regularly until you don't have to think about them before you make your swing.

POSTURE

Correct posture is vital. Just watch the top players on TV. Although the world's great golfers may swing the club differently, they all have identical posture at address when they are preparing to strike the ball.

Before you take up your posture, hold your club in your right hand and place the clubhead behind the ball, check that you are aiming the clubhead correctly and take your grip on the club. Use a 6, 7 or 8 iron as these three clubs are all easy to swing.

There are three stages on the path to correct posture. The first is your stance – where you place your feet when you address the ball. The two other stages involve your knees and back.

POSTURE AT ADDRESS
Flex your knees and stick your bottom out slightly. Your hands should lie directly below your chin. The angle of your back allows your shoulders to rotate easily. Keep your chin up so it is clear of your left shoulder during the backswing.

FROM THE FRONT
Your left arm, your hands and the clubhead can be joined by an imaginary straight line. The ball is in the centre of your stance and your hands are slightly ahead of the ball.

THE RIGHT STANCE

Your feet should be as far apart as your shoulders are wide. In other words you take up a shoulder-width stance. They should also be at a slight outwards angle. The best way to get your feet at the correct angle is to imagine you are standing on the centre of a big clockface. Your right foot should point to 1 o'clock and your left to 11 o'clock.

Once your feet are in the right place, lift the club off the ground, and stand upright and at ease, with your legs straight. Now go on to the next stage.

Keeping your legs straight, bend your torso so that you are leaning forwards with your weight on the balls of your feet.

Finally, bend your knees slightly and let your bottom stick out. This should straighten your back. A straight back at the correct angle to the vertical allows your body to rotate properly when you make your swing.

This final stage also moves your body weight back from the balls of your feet to a more central position. You should always be comfortable and balanced when you have correct posture.

ALIGNMENT

Correct alignment means lining up your body parallel to the ball-to-target line. This may sound easy, but very few golfers achieve it or realize its importance in making sure the ball goes straight and accurately to the target.

Too many golfers take up what they feel is the ideal grip and posture without understanding the correct alignment procedure. Preparation for a shot is as vital as making the stroke itself.

BALL-TO-TARGET LINE

Before aligning yourself for a shot, you must first re-check your aim so that your clubface is square on

Hands below your chin
To check your hand position, try tying a small weight to the end of a piece of string, about 2ft (60cm) long. Grip the other end between your teeth and let the weight hang freely. The string should pass along the same line as your grip.

THE CORRECT POSTURE

1 POSITION OF FEET
Your feet at address must be the same width apart as your shoulders. They should also point slightly outwards.

2 LEAN FORWARD
Stand at ease with your legs straight then lean forward so that your weight is on the balls of your feet. Place the clubhead squarely behind the ball.

TRAINING ALIGNMENT

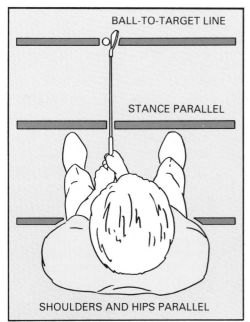

BALL-TO-TARGET LINE

STANCE PARALLEL

SHOULDERS AND HIPS PARALLEL

ALIGN YOUR BODY
Alignment can be surprisingly hard to get right. Your shoulders, especially, must not point at the target but must be parallel to the ball-to-target line.

ON TRACK
One tried and tested way to achieve perfect alignment is to imagine a railway track between your ball and the target. The ball and clubhead are on the far rail, which runs to the base of the target, while the tips of your toes touch the nearside rail. Align your shoulders, hips and knees so that they are parallel to this nearside rail.

3 BEND YOUR KNEES
Bend your knees and stick your bottom out slightly. This straightens your back. Add the correct grip. The club should rest firmly on the ground.

RAILWAY FORMATION
You can make the imaginary railway line idea clearer by placing a number of clubs on the ground in railway line formation. Line up your clubface square on to the club furthest away from you, while taking a stance parallel to the near line. Although your feet and body point left of target, they are in fact correctly placed: parallel to the ball-to-target line.

to the ball-to-target line. It's essential to remember that your body must be parallel to this line. To help do this, imagine another line running between the tips of your big toes.

This line should run parallel to the ball-to-target line. Your knees, hips and shoulders must also be parallel to this new line running from toe to toe.

It might feel as if your shoulders are aiming left of the target but remember you strike the ball with the clubface. Aligning your shoulders *parallel* to the ball-to-target line is vital for creating the perfect swing.

Aligning your shoulders so they point *at* the target is a common fault which makes the club aim too far right. It often occurs when a golfer lines up a shot by looking at the target over the left shoulder. Avoid it by rotating – rather than lifting – your head to check that your clubface is aimed properly. Check your aim several times before you play a stroke that is square to the ball-to-target line.

PRACTISING AIM AND ALIGNMENT

1 VIEW FROM BEHIND
First, view the shot from behind – it's easier to find the intended line of flight. Pick out a marker such as a divot 3ft (1m) beyond the ball on the target line.

2 AIM THE CLUBFACE
Holding the club in your right hand, place the clubhead on the ground behind the ball and aim it square on to the selected marker.

3 TAKE A PARALLEL STANCE
Take a stance parallel to the ball-to-marker line, and grip the club correctly using both hands. Keep the ball central in your stance.

Practise this routine regularly until it becomes as natural as walking. Remember, you must always find the correct alignment before you consider playing the shot.

Ball position and the swing

The last of the five pre-swing essentials to know before learning about the swing is where you place the ball in relation to your feet when you are using the various clubs.

In the normal golf swing, the clubface must be square on to the ball-to-target line at impact. Knowing what goes on during the swing and what happens to the clubface during the swing helps you to get your clubface square on to the ball-to-target line at impact.

CLUB AND STANCE

Depending on the type of club, you stand with your feet further or closer apart. Once you've decided how far apart your feet should be you can then go on and accurately position your ball.

The longer the shaft of your club, the wider apart you have your feet. So your stance is wider for the longer irons such as a 2 or 3 iron and a driver and is narrower for the shorter clubs such as the 8 or 9 irons and the wedges. With a 2 iron,

for instance, your stance should be about as wide as a normal walking pace is long. With a short iron such as a sand wedge you stand with your feet about half as far apart as for a long iron. With a 6 or 7 iron your feet are about shoulder width apart.

PLACING THE BALL

The general rule is: the shorter the shaft, the more central the ball should be in your stance. If you are using a 9 iron, position the ball in the centre of your stance. With a 2 iron, place the ball opposite the inside of your left heel.

For the clubs in between, place the ball between these two positions. When using a medium iron, for instance, place the ball midway between the centre of your stance and the inside of your left heel.

The length of each club's shaft

PLACEMENT AND STANCE
Correct placement is determined by the club you are using. With a medium iron such as a 7 iron, the ball should be placed on a line midway between the inside of your left heel and the centre of your stance. The width of a 7-iron stance is just over half the length of a normal walking stride.

also determines how far away from the ball that you stand. For a long-shafted club such as a 2 iron the ball is further away from you than for a shorter-shafted, high-numbered club.

POSTURE AND SWING PLANE

The ball is placed in these different positions because of the changes to posture brought about by the length of the differing clubs. The shorter the shaft, the nearer you are to the ball, the narrower your stance and the more your back is bent.

It is the angle of your back at address that influences swing plane. The more bent it is the steeper your swing plane. With a longer-shafted club, such as a 2 iron, the ball is further from your feet than with a 9

iron. Your hands are higher and your back is more upright. This automatically creates a flatter swing plane around your body.

The shape of your swing affects the angle at which the clubhead hits the ball, and dictates the amount and type of spin. The steep swing plane of the 9 iron creates backspin, while the flatter plane of the 2 iron produces overspin. Backspin prevents the ball running as far as normal on landing, while overspin increases roll.

SWING PATH

During a correct swing the club-head travels in a path from the inside of the ball-to-target line, briefly along the ball-to-target line at impact and then back inside the ball-to-target line after impact. It

THE SWING

1 TAKEAWAY
In the first 6-9in (15-23cm) of the backswing, the club moves in a straight line. It has yet to be influenced by your upper body.

CLUBS, POSTURE AND PLACEMENT

● BALL OPPOSITE INSIDE LEFT HEEL

● BALL MID-WAY BETWEEN LEFT HEEL AND CENTRE OF STANCE

● BALL IN CENTRE OF STANCE

3 IRON (LONG IRON)
Your back is slightly bent at address and the width of your stance is equal to the length of a normal walking stride. Place the ball opposite the inside of your left heel.

7 IRON (MEDIUM IRON)
The shaft is shorter so your feet are closer together and your back is more bent. The ball is placed closer to your feet and positioned midway between the centre of your stance and opposite your inside left heel.

SAND WEDGE (SHORT IRON)
At address, your back is more bent than it is with either a long or medium iron. The ball is closer to your feet and is placed in the centre of your stance.

2 NATURAL ROTATION
By the mid-point of the backswing the body rotation moves the club inside the ball-to-target line. This also opens the clubface.

3 THE HIGHEST POINT
Near the top of the backswing, the club continues its path around the body. At the top, the shaft of the club should be parallel with the target.

4 DOWNSWING
The downswing is almost identical to the backswing. The club follows a path inside the ball-to-target line and the clubface closes.

5 SQUARE CONTACT
The clubface gradually returns, from being open at the start of the downswing, to being perfectly square to the ball-to-target line at impact. The club travels briefly along the ball-to-target line at impact.

6 THROUGHSWING
On the throughswing, the club continues along its path and moves back inside the ball-to-target line. The clubface continues to rotate and gradually closes as the throughswing continues.

never goes outside the ball-to-target line.

At the start of the backswing, turning your body moves the clubhead inside the ball-to-target line. It also causes the clubface to open and, at the mid-point of the backswing, its face has opened so that it is at an angle of 90° to the ball-to-target line.

CLUBFACE AT IMPACT

During the downswing and right up to impact the clubhead gradually closes and only at one brief moment – impact – is the clubface square to the ball-to-target line. On the throughswing the face continues to rotate and closes.

SWING PLANES

A perfect in-to-in swing path alone does not guarantee square contact. The ball must also be correctly placed in relation to your stance. Golf is often said to be a game of inches. One inch off target on the tee can mean 10-15 yards off line down the fairway.

When the ball is too far back in the stance, the club meets it too early on the downswing. The clubface is still open and, even with the correct in-to-in swing path, the ball goes to the right of target.

If the ball is too far forward in the stance, the club makes contact too late (on the throughswing). The clubface has closed slightly and the ball lands left of target.

3 IRON

7 IRON

It's easier to place the ball correctly once you understand each club's swing plane. The swing plane for a 3 iron (pink) is flatter than that of a shorter 7 iron (green). Your spine is more upright and produces a sweeping action around your body, with the clubhead reaching its lowest point at a later stage in the swing path. The ball is therefore placed further forward in the stance than for the 7 iron.

pro tip

Toeing the line
To help understand the opening and closing of the clubface during the swing path, slowly swing the club back and through the normal swing plane. At the mid-point on both the backswing and the throughswing, the toe of the club should point directly at the sky. At these points, the face should also be open by 90° and closed by 90° respectively.

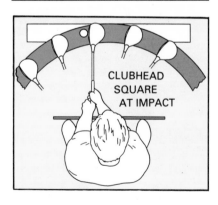

CLUBHEAD SQUARE AT IMPACT

IN-TO-IN CLUBHEAD
During the correct in-to-in swing path, the clubhead should never move outside the ball-to-target line. Note how the clubface is square to the target at one point only – impact.

Shaping the swing

The aim of all golfers is to develop a simple, repeatable swing. The fewer individual movements there are in your swing, the less parts there are to go wrong and the better chance you have of repeating it.

When building a swing it is vital to understand how different parts of the body work together. Your head, shoulders, arms, hands, hips, knees and feet, must interact correctly if you are to swing efficiently. A good swing is the result of co-ordinated body rotation, and not a collection of separate movements.

SWING EXERCISE

Practise this exercise several times a week to help you develop correct body rotation, flexibility and freedom of movement. Hold the club behind your shoulders with both hands, and take up a normal middle-iron address position. Make sure your feet are the correct distance apart.

KEEP YOUR HEAD CENTRAL

Your head is the centre of any swing, and influences the movement of every other part of the body. By keeping a central position throughout, your head helps you to return the clubhead to its precise starting point. Your shoulders turn around your head. This sparks off hip rotation, which in turn begins leg movement.

TAKEAWAY AND BACKSWING

From the address position, where you have set your aim, taken grip, adopted the right posture, aligned your body and placed the ball correctly, you can start the take-away – the beginning of the backswing.

For the first 6-9in (15-23cm) of the takeaway, the club moves in a straight line as the left arm triggers the backswing. The base of the clubhead keeps quite close to the ground. Your left arm pulls the left shoulder under your chin. From here, body rotation begins to shape the swing as it coils up the power.

Your right arm must stay relaxed, so it can fold under the influence of your rotating left shoulder. This shoulder continues to be pulled around – although it stays on the same plane. It must stay level and not dip or rise during any part of the swing.

Move your head
The old saying, 'keep your head still', should not be taken literally. Although your head mustn't sway, the natural movement of your body means it has to revolve slightly during backswing and downswing, and more on the throughswing. Head rotation should co-ordinate with shoulder action. Holding your head rigid prevents correct body rotation and could even injure you.

ROTATE TO THE RIGHT
Rotate your body to the right, making sure your shoulders stay on the same plane (level). From an even distribution at the start, your weight transfers to the inside of your right foot. At this point your back should face the target. Your right knee stays flexed throughout the backswing.

RETURN TO CENTRE
Your left hip starts the movement that returns the body to a central position. The rotating hip triggers your left shoulder, which also revolves to the left. You are now in a position similar to your starting point. When you begin your followthrough, think of it as a reversal of your backswing.

CHEST FACES TARGET
Your shoulders continue to rotate to the left. By the end of the exercise your chest and head should face the target, with your weight on the outside of your left foot. Your left knee stays flexed on the throughswing. This exercise trains the various parts of the body to work together.

BUILDING YOUR SWING

1 STARTING THE BACKSWING
From address (inset) the club moves in a straight line for the first 6-9in (15-23cm) of the takeaway – staying close to the ground. This action pulls your left shoulder to the right, as you begin your backswing.

2 LEFT SHOULDER PULLED UNDER CHIN
Your left shoulder continues to be pulled under your chin and at the two-thirds point of the backswing is almost directly under your chin. Your wrists hinge naturally, caused by the passage of the club.

3 TOP OF THE BACKSWING
At the top of the backswing your shoulders have rotated 90° and your hips 45°. The shaft points at the target and is parallel to the ground. Your left knee is flexed and most of your weight is on the inside of your right foot.

4 STARTING THE DOWNSWING
Your left hip starts the downswing by turning to the left. This action must be smooth, pulling your arms and hands into the proper striking position. Don't turn your hip too soon or the club moves outside the in-to-in path.

As your shoulders rotate, they pull your hips in the same direction. The hips must also remain on the same plane. But they must be flexible enough to let your body weight shift from an even distribution at address, over to the right foot by the mid-point on the backswing.

By the top of the backswing, your shoulders should have turned 90° and your hips 45°. The shaft of the club points towards the target and is parallel to the ground. Most of your weight is on the inside of your right foot, with the right leg flexed.

DOWNSWING AND IMPACT

The start of the downswing must be smooth and unhurried. It is triggered by the left hip which starts rotating back to its original address position. This action pulls your hands and arms into a position where they can swing freely through the ball.

After impact, your right shoulder continues to pull the hips to the left, which in turn rotates the right leg. As your right shoulder rotates

to its final followthrough position, it turns your head around. This is a natural movement. If you force your head to stay still after impact, you prevent your body completing the correct followthrough movement.

By the completion of the swing, your body should have rotated to face the target, with the weight transferred to your left foot.

YOUR ARMS AND HANDS

Let your arms and hands swing naturally. They should be passive during the stroke and influenced only by the rotation of the swing. They do not shape the swing.

Many beginners wrongly believe that as the arms and hands are in direct contact with the club, they alone control the swing.

If you move your hands and arms independently from the rest of your body, they swing back and through impact in various directions and it is difficult to develop the correct in-to-in swingpath. You must have co-ordinated body rotation so that you'll be able to develop a consistent, repeatable and accurate swing.

THE HALF SWING

To help you build your full swing, try practising the half swing, in which you finish the backswing and throughswing at the two-thirds position of the full swing.

Feel these key movements: your left shoulder being pulled under your chin; the clubhead's weight pulling your right shoulder and hands into impact; your face and chest turning to the target after impact; correct weight transfer.

pro tip

Mirror image
Looking in a mirror is an excellent way to check your swing – but make sure you are out of reach of furniture, glass and lights. If you have a large mirror at home, you can watch yourself build a swing and compare the way you are moving to the sequence on these pages. This way you can check that you are building your swing properly. Alternatively, use the reflection from a large window.

5 IMPACT AND FOLLOWTHROUGH
At impact your left arm, hands and the clubhead form a straight line and your weight moves on to your left foot. On the followthrough your right shoulder is pulled to the left.

6 THE END OF THE SWING
Most of your weight is transferred on to the outside of your left foot by the end of the swing. Your left knee remains slightly flexed and your chest is square to the target. Your head has revolved to face the target.

HOW YOUR HEAD MOVES

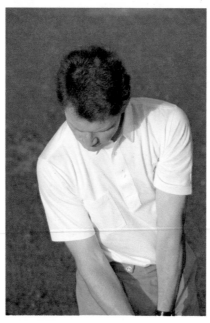

1 BACKSWING
Your neck muscles must be relaxed enough to let your head revolve. Your head turns slightly to the right, affected by shoulder turn, but it mustn't tilt up or down.

2 IMPACT
As the club moves back to impact, your head returns to the same position it was in at address. This occurs naturally with the movement of the swing.

3 THROUGHSWING
As your right shoulder continues to turn to the left after impact, your head automatically comes up. Head movement must be natural or it restricts followthrough.

HALF SWING

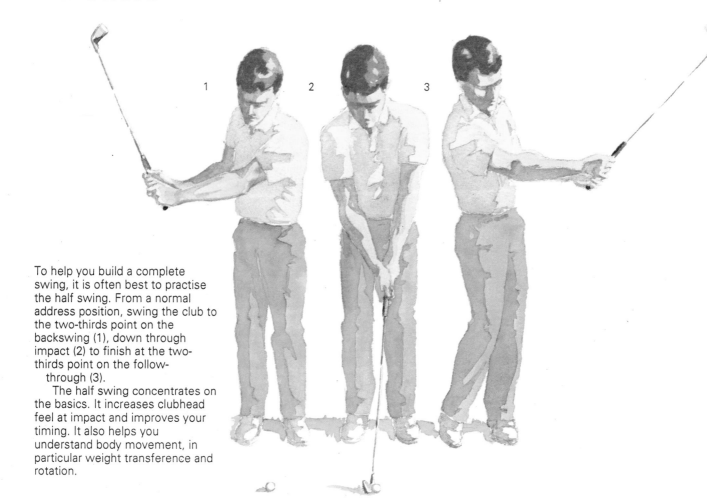

To help you build a complete swing, it is often best to practise the half swing. From a normal address position, swing the club to the two-thirds point on the backswing (1), down through impact (2) to finish at the two-thirds point on the follow-through (3).

The half swing concentrates on the basics. It increases clubhead feel at impact and improves your timing. It also helps you understand body movement, in particular weight transference and rotation.

The nine strikes

Finding out the cause of a fault in your swing is much easier if you develop an understanding of how the clubface strikes the ball.

If you spray the ball to all points of the compass, don't simply curse your luck and move on. Ask yourself why your shots fly off target.

You can strike a golf ball in nine different ways – some desirable, others disastrous. Whatever you intend with your shot, one of those nine is sure to dictate its flight path.

When you can assess precisely which one of the nine is responsible for each shot, you find the root of any swing problem more quickly.

The two vital factors in deciding the ball's fate after impact are your swing path and the clubface position at impact – assuming that you strike with the centre of the clubface.

The immediate direction of the ball is caused by the swing path of the club. Its direction for the rest of the shot is determined by the angle of the clubface at impact – open, closed or square – in relation to the ball-to-target line.

HIT STRAIGHT FIRST

The greatest golfers play with different styles, but they all agree on one point: the hardest shot in golf is the straight one.

For this reason, some draw the ball, others prefer to fade – but very few set out to play straight. To rely on consistent straight hitting is risky.

Straight hitting is hard because golf balls are designed to take up spin – it helps them to rise, to stop and to roll. Sidespin is also easy to apply. If you apply the correct amount of sidespin – by changing your alignment – you fade and draw the ball. Too much sidespin causes a slice or a hook.

Set your mind on hitting the ball straight before you start working on draws and fades. Concentrate on achieving an in-to-in path with a square clubface at impact by setting up parallel to the ball-to-target line.

There's a small margin of difference between a deliberate fade and a damaging slice. Only when you know how to take sidespin off the ball can you add it intentionally.

NINE POSSIBLE PATHS

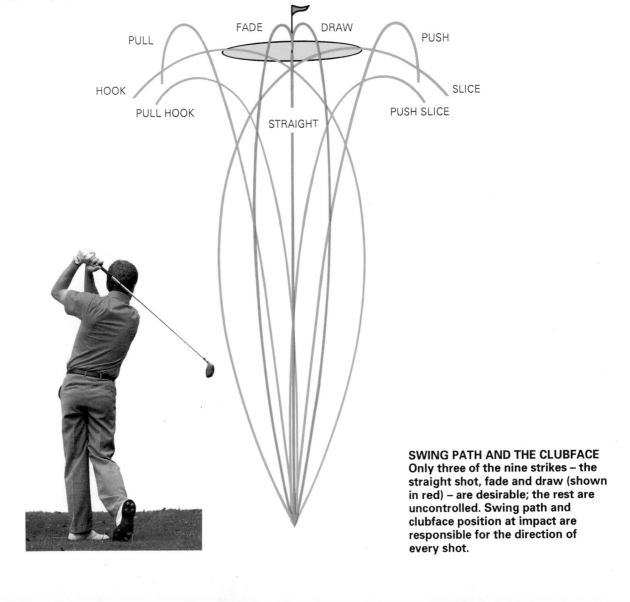

SWING PATH AND THE CLUBFACE
Only three of the nine strikes – the straight shot, fade and draw (shown in red) – are desirable; the rest are uncontrolled. Swing path and clubface position at impact are responsible for the direction of every shot.

IN-TO-OUT SWING PATH

OUT TO IN

PATH OF BALL

BALL-TO-TARGET LINE

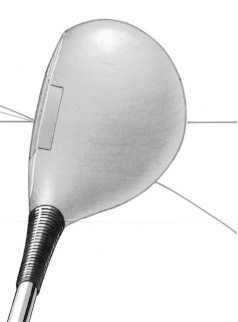

OPEN CLUBFACE

✗ **PUSH**
The club travels from inside the ball-to-target line to outside, and the clubface is open at impact. The ball travels immediately right of target in a straight line.

✗ **SLICE**
The clubhead comes from outside to inside the line, with an open clubface at impact. The ball starts left of target before curving sharply to the right.

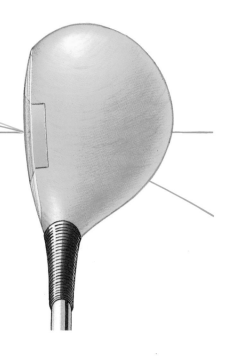

SQUARE CLUBFACE

✔ **DRAW**
Widely regarded as the ideal golf shot – because it combines distance and accuracy – the draw flies slightly right before returning to centre. It happens when the clubface meets the ball square to the ball-to-target line on an in-to-out path.

✔ **FADE**
The fade starts left of target and returns to centre, stopping quickly. The clubface is square at impact, travelling on an out-to-in path.

✗ **HOOK**
The ball starts straight – or slightly right – and curves violently left, because the clubhead has passed along an in-to-out path with the clubface closed at impact.

✗ **PULL**
The out-to-in swing path combines with the closed clubface to send the ball immediately left of target in a straight line.

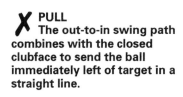

CLOSED CLUBFACE

IN TO IN

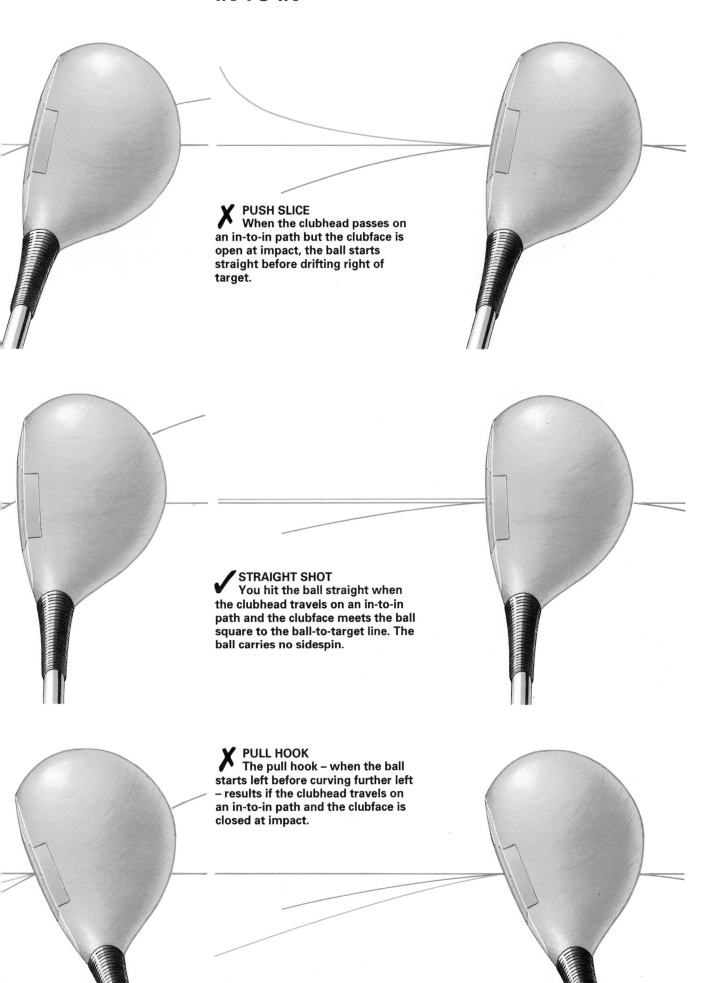

✗ PUSH SLICE
When the clubhead passes on an in-to-in path but the clubface is open at impact, the ball starts straight before drifting right of target.

✓ STRAIGHT SHOT
You hit the ball straight when the clubhead travels on an in-to-in path and the clubface meets the ball square to the ball-to-target line. The ball carries no sidespin.

✗ PULL HOOK
The pull hook – when the ball starts left before curving further left – results if the clubhead travels on an in-to-in path and the clubface is closed at impact.

pro tip

Out to in for sand play

Although you should normally try to achieve an in-to-in swing path with your straight tee, fairway and green shots, accurate greenside bunker play requires an out-to-in swing path.

The ball must normally gain height and stop quickly. Square the blade to the ball-to-target line and open your stance – this provides the extra loft you need. Your stance creates an out-to-in swing path, and the clubface is square at impact.

Keep it square when putting

If you ever struggle for accuracy on the green, always remember to return to the basics – the swing path and position of the clubface should be consistent when you're putting.

All putts are straight – the clubhead should always travel straight along the line of your putt. The clubface must be square to that line at impact, and on shorter putts should be square to it throughout the stroke.

Because of the extra backswing and throughswing needed for long putts, the path of your pendulum swing can be slightly in to in.

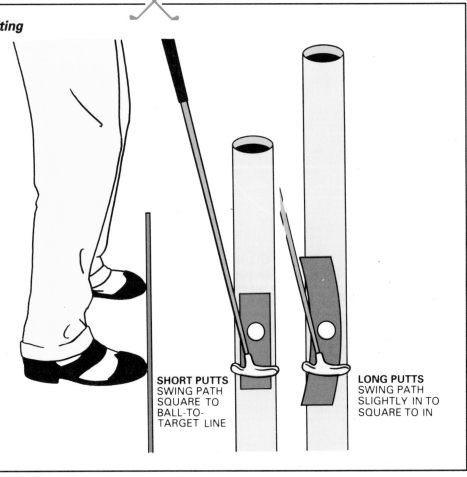

SHORT PUTTS SWING PATH SQUARE TO BALL-TO-TARGET LINE

LONG PUTTS SWING PATH SLIGHTLY IN TO SQUARE TO IN

Pre-shot routine

Learn and use a good pre-shot routine to eliminate the faults that can occur before you make any strike. Correct preparation helps you to become more consistent, which in turn lowers your score.

The pre-shot routine is a blend of mental and physical stages that leads you to the right position and frame of mind to hit the ball where you want it to go. You should build a consistent pre-shot routine into your game at an early stage.

The physical aspects of it – where you achieve the correct address position through a series of actions – are usually quite easy to pick up and perform.

The mental aspects – visualizing where you want the ball to go and then deciding on the type of stroke you want to play – can be a bit hard at first. But visualizing does improve with experience and in the long run is the key to lower scores.

The visualizing aspect of your pre-shot routine begins the moment you walk on to the tee, or

ASSESSING THE SHOT

Pre-shot routine starts as you approach the ball or teeing off area and assess the factors involved in making the shot.

DISTANCE
Try to judge the distance between your ball and the target – use a distance chart if there is one.

HAZARDS
Make a mental note of the hazards that lie between your ball and the target, such as the bunker and rough here. Check the position of the pin, and look for any slopes.

WEATHER AND COURSE CONDITIONS
Find out the direction and strength of the wind – if there is any – and assess the condition of both the fairway and green. Are they damp, dry or even bone hard? The state of the ground affects the amount of roll on the ball.

CHOOSE YOUR CLUB
Choose the best club for the stroke from your knowledge of distance, hazards, and the probable effect of weather and course conditions.

SHAPE THE SHOT
Decide on the best line to the target. Is it right, left, or centre? Your choice of club might affect the decision. A high shot can clear hazards, while a low running shot doesn't. Visualize the ball's path.

FEEL THE SWING
Picture and feel the stroke in your mind before making a few practice swings.

PREPARING TO HIT

1 STAND BEHIND THE BALL
Stand behind the ball and select your ball-to-target line. Pick a small mark (such as a divot hole, leaf or twig) on that line, no more than a club's length from your ball.

2 AIM THE CLUBFACE
Hold the club in your right hand and place the clubhead behind the ball. Aim the clubface square on to the ball-to-mark-to-target line.

when you reach your ball on the fairway.

PREPARING TO VISUALIZE

Visualizing is a two-part process: assessing the difficulty of the shot by studying the hazards and course conditions, and deciding on the type of stroke you want to play so that you can set about shaping the shot in your mind.

If you are new to golf, you may find it difficult to visualize. Although assessment of hazards and course conditions is quite easy to grasp, deciding on the shape of your shot takes a little longer to perfect.

ASSESS THE PROBLEMS

You have to assess a number of factors. You can't just walk up to the ball, take a swipe at it and hope it goes the correct distance and in the right direction.

First, judge the distance your ball is from the target – whether this is a flag on the green or a

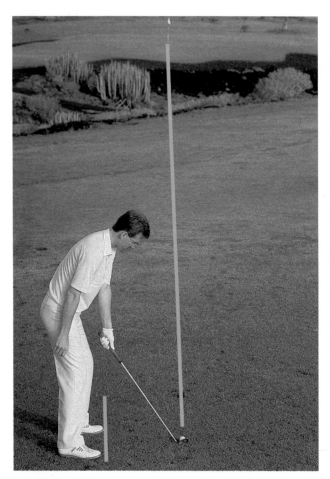

3 TAKE A PARALLEL STANCE
Align your feet and body parallel to the ball-to-mark-to-target line, and adopt the ideal posture. Take the correct grip with your left hand.

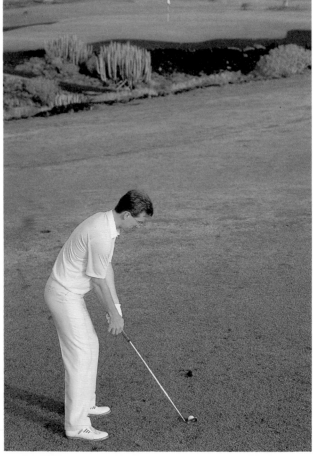

4 COMPLETE THE GRIP
Add your right hand to the club to complete the grip. Check that the clubface is still aimed square on to the ball-to-mark-to-target line.

position on the fairway. Make a mental note of the hazards that come into play, such as out-of-bounds posts, ditches, trees, bunkers and streams. Also note exactly where the pin is and any fairway slopes.

Second, assess weather and course conditions as these dictate which club you should use. Check for wind, its direction and strength. Is the fairway or green damp or dry and how is the ball likely to run? Even when playing from familiar tees and fairways, you need to re-assess club selection because of changing conditions.

When you have analysed hazards and conditions, select your club.

SHAPING THE SHOT

Now decide on the type of shot you want to play, and imagine the intended flight path of the ball. To visualize the path of the ball, you must shape the shot. For example, if all the trouble is on the right side

of the fairway, it is best to play down the left. If the fairway is narrow, you might want to use an iron, not a wood, from the tee for accuracy.

Visualize the ball travelling through the air, landing on the green or fairway, and rolling towards the target.

The key to shaping your shot is knowing your capabilities. You must know the distance you can hit with each club and understand the flight path of the ball in each shot. The average player hits a wedge shot between 100 and 110yd (90 and 100m), with a 10yd (9m) difference between each successive club.

As your swing develops and your timing improves, your game becomes more consistent and it is easier to judge the distance you achieve with each club. Your swing must be repeatable. Inconsistency creeps in if your tempo varies from shot to shot.

Your tempo has to remain the same before you can develop a feel for distance. Only when you know

the level of your own ability can you attempt to shape the shot.

Once you have shaped your shot, 'feel' the swing in your mind before removing the chosen club from your bag. Then take a couple of practice swings.

Learning to visualize your shots takes experience, so don't worry if

Don't be rushed

Never rush your pre-shot routine. Hurrying your preparation leads to a quick, jerky stroke. Stay relaxed and calm at all times. Then you can maintain a smooth rhythm and tempo from the moment you start visualizing your shot, through to pre-shot routine and to making the stroke itself. Be deliberate and remember there is no time limit for playing a shot. If you feel tension creeping into your grip, lift the club off the ground and jiggle it.

5 REMOVE TENSION
Lift the club off the ground and waggle it in your hands. Move your feet at the same time to release tension. Check your aim by looking at the target.

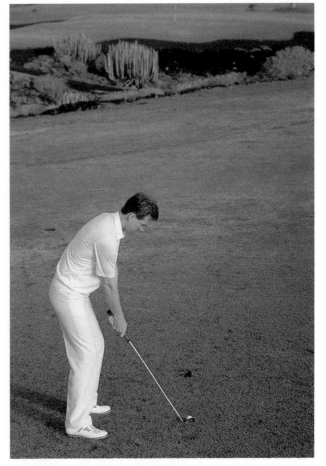

6 FINAL ADDRESS POSITION
The pre-shot routine is now complete and you're in a position to play the shot. Careful preparation is the key to a correct swing and successful shot.

on the first few occasions it is very much a case of trial and error.

PREPARING TO HIT

Having selected your club and decided on the type of shot you want to play, you now have to adopt the correct address position by following a number of stages.

This routine builds up the correct grip, posture and alignment and puts you in a relaxed and confident frame of mind. It gives you the best possible chance of making a good stroke. As with the visualizing stages of the pre-shot routine, you must go through these physical stages every time you play a shot, whether on tee or fairway.

BALL-TO-TARGET LINE

Stand behind the ball and select your intended ball-to-target line. Choose a small mark, such as a twig, leaf or divot hole, about a club's length in front of the ball and on that same ball-to-target line.

Hold the club in your right hand, and place the sole of the clubhead behind the ball, aiming the clubface square on to the mark. Then stand parallel to the ball-to-marker line and adopt the correct posture. Your knees, hips and shoulders must also be parallel to this line. Add the correct grip, before checking that the clubface is still aimed properly.

Rid yourself of any tension by lifting the club off the ground and waggling it in your hands. Move your feet up and down in sympathy. This relaxes your body and muscles, and allows you to swing freely and correctly. Tension creeps in at address when the body becomes rigid. You have to remove it before you make any stroke.

A consistent pre-shot routine is as important as the swing itself.

How much wind?
To detect the amount of wind, throw a few blades of grass into the air above your head and see where and how fast they are blown. You may need to repeat this action to confirm wind strength and direction. Club selection varies considerably in windy conditions.

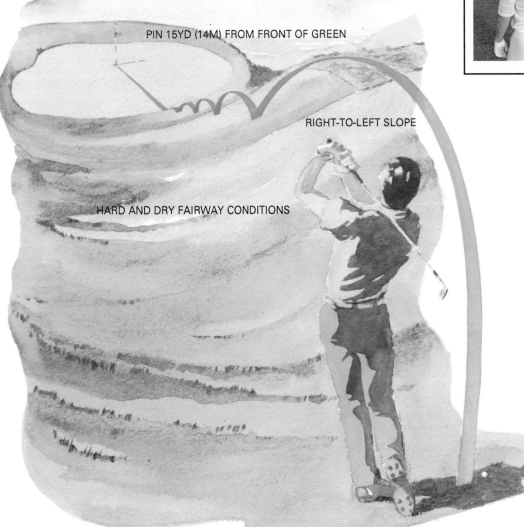

PIN 15YD (14M) FROM FRONT OF GREEN

RIGHT-TO-LEFT SLOPE

HARD AND DRY FAIRWAY CONDITIONS

BALL 160YD (146M) FROM PIN

Imagine the ball's path
Try to imagine the ball's flight, where you expect it to land and how it might run. This golfer's ball is 160yd (146m) from the flag, there are no hazards, but there is a right-to-left slope. There is no wind and the surface of the fairway is hard and dry.

He chooses a 7 iron for the shot, as he intends to land the ball about 20yd (18m) from the green. Because the slope is from right to left, he aims his shot about 15yd (14m) right of the pin. The slope will then carry his ball towards the flag. He completes his final practice swing and is now ready to make the stroke.

Swing Triggers

Too many amateurs are scared of starting their swing for fear of making poor moves and hitting a bad shot. Much of this fear stems from too stiff and static an address that's full of tension.

Starting the swing from a totally motionless position makes it hard to take the club away smoothly and find good rhythm. Standing too still can lead you to freeze over the ball. There should always be some part of your body moving slightly to avoid freezing – even if it's just a tiny shift of weight from foot to foot. This relieves tension.

HABIT FORMING

To help start the swing in a confident and repeatable fashion every time, you can develop a habit of moving the same part of your body just before you take the club away. If this trigger is harnessed to a good takeaway your whole swing becomes more consistent. It's encouraging to know that when you make this trigger move your backswing should start properly.

Many of the world's top players have some little manoeuvre that starts their swing, but there is no hard and fast rule of what it should be – it's personal taste. It can be with your hands, legs or head, and may be a tiny or quite noticeable movement. But it must be natural.

Jack Nicklaus gives the club a quick squeeze, while others push their hands forward just before they start. Both Gary Player and

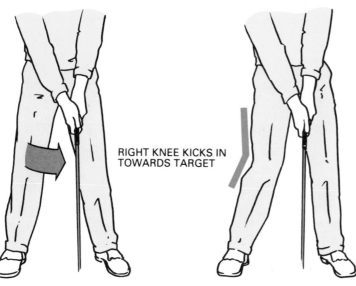

RIGHT KNEE KICKS IN TOWARDS TARGET

KNEE KICK
Take note of Australian Rodger Davis' swing, particularly the deliberate pushing of his right knee towards the target just before he starts his stroke. At an easy pace his knee moves about 2in (5cm), giving him the stimulus to start his swing. His right leg is then set and acts as a brace, around which he can turn fully into a powerful backswing position.

Rodger Davis kick the right knee in towards the left but in different ways. Player's knee action is fast and looks almost involuntary, while Davis' is slower and even appears calculated. It shows that there's no proper or correct way of performing it – both players do what works for them.

Nick Faldo flexes his knees immediately before his takeaway, triggering the most consistent swing in golf. Because his swing is based on such a solid stance the movement is slight.

But a word of caution. Whatever you try, be sure not to become too reliant on it. Having a helping hand to start your swing with rhythm doesn't mean you can neglect your full swing. Go on working on perfecting your swing, using a starting trigger as an effective grooving aid.

pro tip

PUSH HANDS FORWARD SLIGHTLY JUST BEFORE STROKE

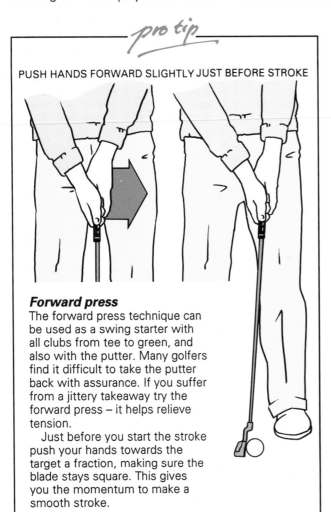

Forward press

The forward press technique can be used as a swing starter with all clubs from tee to green, and also with the putter. Many golfers find it difficult to take the putter back with assurance. If you suffer from a jittery takeaway try the forward press – it helps relieve tension.

Just before you start the stroke push your hands towards the target a fraction, making sure the blade stays square. This gives you the momentum to make a smooth stroke.

FALDO'S FLEX

Since Nick Faldo has been working with David Leadbetter, his swing has changed dramatically. Nick's willowy action has been transformed into a solid, compact swing. He now starts his stroke with a small flex of the knees. This creates the momentum to move easily and smoothly into his backswing with a free leg action and the club on perfect plane.

SMALL KNEE FLEX HELPS START SWING SMOOTHLY

masterclass

McNulty's move

Zimbabwe's Mark McNulty is one of the few top golfers who activates the swing with a move of his head. After setting up he makes a slow deliberate turn of his head to the right, and then starts his swing.

This not only gives McNulty the impetus to begin his swing but also provides a pivot around which he can turn fully and still keep a steady head throughout the stroke.

One of the most consistent golfers in the world, Mark also uses the forward press when putting. Both the head move and his press have helped him develop an excellent swing and putting touch.

Using woods

You use the woods for maximum distance both on the tee and the fairway. Although woods are usually harder to control than irons, especially when you are new to the game, you should learn how to use them as soon as possible. Using woods to hit the ball long distances is an ability you must learn at an early stage to lower your scores.

A well-struck wood shot sets you up in the best possible way for the remainder of the hole.

The most commonly used woods are the 1, 3 and 5. They are designed to increase your distance and power without any extra effort.

While the size and shape of the clubhead provides the most obvious visual difference between woods and irons, it is the length of their shafts that helps you achieve the extra distance.

Shape, material and length combine with your technique to extract power from the club.

MORE POWER

When you swing a wood, the longer shaft gives a wider arc and this means that the clubhead has a greater distance to travel. If you swing a wood with the same rhythm and tempo as an iron, the clubhead travels around the arc in the same time, but it has to cover much more distance and this raises its speed. It is this increase in clubhead speed that provides you with the additional power to hit the ball longer dis-

WOOD AND IRON SWINGPLANES

SWINGPLANE OF IRON

SWINGPLANE OF WOOD

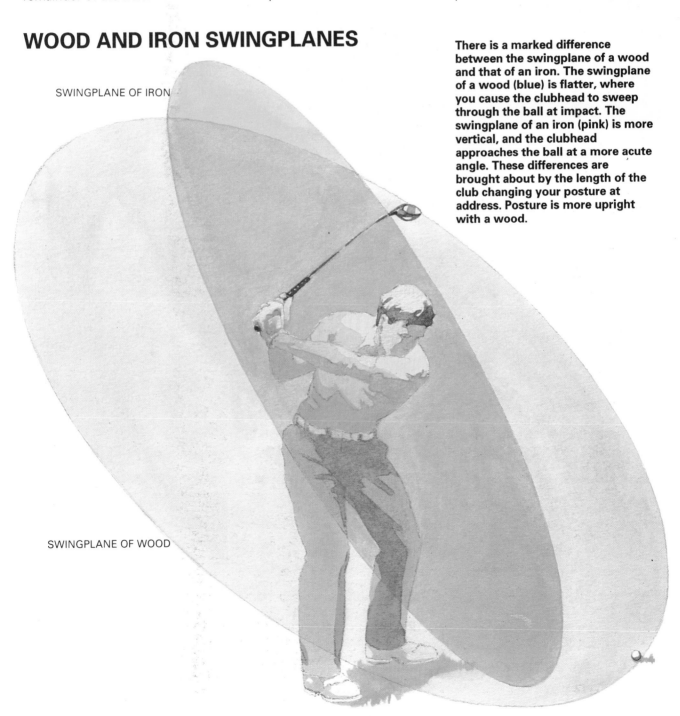

There is a marked difference between the swingplane of a wood and that of an iron. The swingplane of a wood (blue) is flatter, where you cause the clubhead to sweep through the ball at impact. The swingplane of an iron (pink) is more vertical, and the clubhead approaches the ball at a more acute angle. These differences are brought about by the length of the club changing your posture at address. Posture is more upright with a wood.

SWINGING WITH WOODS

1 ADDRESS & TAKEAWAY
At address the ball is opposite the inside of your left heel. Take the club away slowly keeping the clubhead low to the ground.

2 ROTATE TO THE RIGHT
Allow your upper body to rotate freely as your left arm swings the club back. By the two-thirds point in your backswing your weight has transferred from a central position at address to the inside of your right foot.

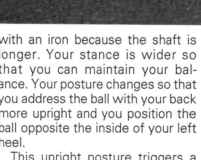

3 TOP OF THE BACKSWING
At the top of the backswing your shoulders have rotated 90° and your hips 45°. Make sure you complete the backswing before starting the downswing – a slight pause before the downswing helps. At the top of the backswing the shaft should point at the target.

tances. You do not have to speed up your swing and tempo to make the clubhead go faster. Your tempo should be the same for every 'full' shot from driving to pitching.

While the longer shaft of the wood should not affect your timing, it does lead to changes in your address including stance, posture and ball position. It also affects your swingplane.

ADDRESS AND SWINGPLANE

With a wood, you stand further away from the ball than you would

with an iron because the shaft is longer. Your stance is wider so that you can maintain your balance. Your posture changes so that you address the ball with your back more upright and you position the ball opposite the inside of your left heel.

This upright posture triggers a number of other differences between woods and irons. Your swingplane is flatter, so the clubhead approaches the ball at a shallower angle. You sweep through the ball, which is struck at a later point in your swing. This is why the ball is placed opposite the inside of your left heel.

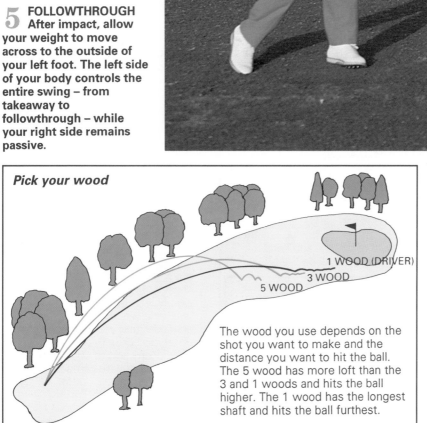

4 STARTING THE DOWNSWING
Rotate your left hip to the left to start the downswing. This pulls your arms and hands into an ideal striking position.

5 FOLLOWTHROUGH
After impact, allow your weight to move across to the outside of your left foot. The left side of your body controls the entire swing – from takeaway to followthrough – while your right side remains passive.

Pick your wood

1 WOOD (DRIVER)
3 WOOD
5 WOOD

The wood you use depends on the shot you want to make and the distance you want to hit the ball. The 5 wood has more loft than the 3 and 1 woods and hits the ball higher. The 1 wood has the longest shaft and hits the ball furthest.

6 THE COMPLETED POSITION
Allow the momentum of your club to pull your right shoulder and your head to face the target. Your whole body should also face the target. At the finish you should be balanced with most of your weight on your left foot.

BALL POSITION AT ADDRESS

FORWARD IN THE STANCE
With a wood, place the ball opposite the inside of your left heel and stand with your feet about as far apart as a normal walking pace is long. With a medium iron the ball is near the middle of your stance.

DISTANCE FROM FEET
Stand further away from the ball when you use a wood than you do with an iron. You have to do this because the shaft of a wood is longer.

THE BACKSWING

Once you have understood the changes to your stance, posture, ball position and swingplane, the basic technique for using woods is similar to using irons. Your tempo remains the same, as do your grip, aim and alignment procedures.

From address, take the club away slowly, keeping the clubhead close to the ground for the first 6-9in (15-23cm). Your left shoulder is pulled across and your weight transfers from an even distribution at address to the inside of your right foot by the completion of the backswing.

PAUSE AT THE TOP

When you reach the top of your backswing, allow for a slight pause before starting the downswing. This pause helps create rhythm and improves timing by separating the backswing from the downswing. Many golfers believe that the backswing and downswing are one continuous movement. This is wrong, and to treat them as one movement only leads to a rushed swing and a poor strike.

THE DOWNSWING

Begin the downswing by smoothly rotating your left hip to the left. This pulls your hands, arms and the clubhead down to the halfway position where your arms and hands swing the clubhead through the ball. The momentum of the clubhead pulls your right shoulder under your chin. Your head rotates to face the target and your weight moves across to your left foot.

TEEING UP THE BALL

When playing a wood shot from a tee peg you have to place the peg at the correct height. The height varies from club to club, but the general rule is that the centre of the ball should be level with the top of the clubface when the club is resting on the ground and the ball is on the tee.

Clubfaces on woods vary in depth, although within any one set, the lower the number of the wood then the deeper its clubface and bigger its clubhead. The 1 wood has the deepest clubface of all woods. The tee peg for a 1 wood should be higher than for a 3 wood, which in turn is higher than for a 5-wood. A ball teed at the correct height is easy to sweep off the top of the tee peg.

If you don't tee your ball at the correct height you lose both distance and accuracy or even mis-hit the shot.

TEEING HEIGHTS

When teeing up, half the ball should be above the top of the clubface at address. So, the deeper the clubface, the higher the tee peg should be set in the ground. Because the 1 wood has a deeper clubface than both the 3 and 5 wood, its tee peg should be

higher. The 5 wood has a shallower clubface so the ball is teed lower.

If you tee-up too high you might hit the ball with the top of the clubhead and send it into the sky. If you tee up too low you might hit the top of the ball and send it a short distance along the ground.

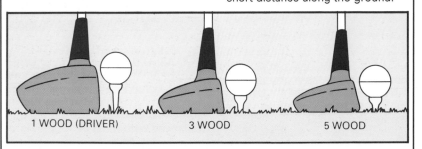

1 WOOD (DRIVER)   3 WOOD   5 WOOD

Practise your driving
It's vital to build a repeatable and consistent stroke with your woods. A long hit with your driver gives you the best possible chance of reaching the green of a long hole in few strokes. Practise with your woods until you are confident that you can hit long distances accurately. If you neglect any part of your game, the whole of your game is bound to suffer.

Fairway woods

Fairway woods – used for distance – are commonly referred to as numbers 2, 3, 4 and 5. Most players carry two – usually a 3 and 5.

There are similarities between a fairway wood and a driver (1 wood). Both hit the ball a long way. The clubhead on both is made from wood, metal or graphite. But fairway woods are designed to hit the ball off the ground and are ideal for your second shot on long par 4s and par 5s.

The clubhead on a fairway wood has a low centre of gravity so that most of its weight hits below the middle of the ball, which helps to propel it upwards.

This is not the case with a driver,

MAXIMUM FAIRWAY DISTANCE
If you need top distance from the fairway take a wood. It is easier to use than a long iron because of its bigger clubface loft and rounded clubhead – which sweeps through impact more smoothly than an iron.

SWINGING A FAIRWAY WOOD

1 **ADDRESS POSITION**
At address the ball is opposite the inside of your left heel and your posture is more upright than normal.

2 **MID BACKSWING**
Rotate your upper body to the right, keeping the clubhead close to the ground for the first 6-9in (15-22cm). Your left arm remains straight for the takeaway.

3 **TOP OF BACKSWING**
At the top of the backswing your upper body has rotated halfway – about 90° – and your lower body about 45°. The club's shaft points at the target.

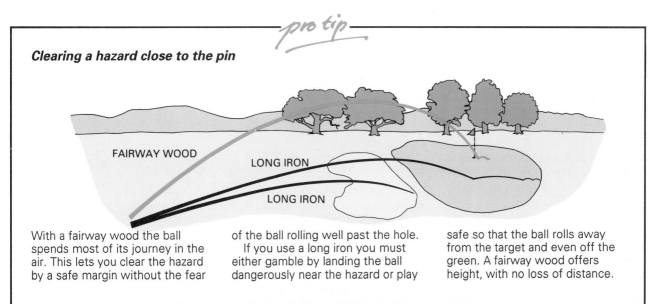

pro tip

Clearing a hazard close to the pin

FAIRWAY WOOD

LONG IRON

LONG IRON

With a fairway wood the ball spends most of its journey in the air. This lets you clear the hazard by a safe margin without the fear of the ball rolling well past the hole.

If you use a long iron you must either gamble by landing the ball dangerously near the hazard or play safe so that the ball rolls away from the target and even off the green. A fairway wood offers height, with no loss of distance.

4 THE DOWNSWING
On the downswing your body starts to uncoil, led by your left hip which rotates to the left. The downswing must be smooth and unhurried.

5 THROUGH IMPACT
The clubhead is swept through the ball by power generated on the downswing. Don't let your head lift up too early on the followthrough.

6 FINAL POSITION
At the end of the swing your upper body and head face the target, with most of your weight on your left foot. Your finish should be balanced and relaxed.

which has a clubhead with a high centre of gravity and is designed to play a raised ball from a tee peg. Don't take a driver from the fairway because most of its weight is above the centre of the ball.

EASY TO USE

The 3 and 5 woods hit the ball about the same distance as the 1 and 2 irons. When faced with a long shot, the high handicap player should choose a wood.

A fairway wood gives much better height than an iron – it has a lower centre of gravity and a bigger clubface loft. The rounded clubhead also sweeps through impact more smoothly than a long iron, especially in the rough.

While long irons give slightly more control when struck perfectly, they are so difficult to use that only low handicap golfers and professionals are skilful enough to play with them. An average player achieves a consistently better strike with a fairway wood.

HEIGHT AND LENGTH

A fairway wood is one of the most versatile clubs in your bag, combining height with length. Not only does it hit the ball as far as a long iron, it also hits it higher.

If your path is blocked by a tall obstacle, such as a tree, hedge or wall, a fairway wood often provides quick enough lift for your ball

The fairway woods

2 WOOD   3 WOOD   4 WOOD   5 WOOD

There are four fairway woods – a 2, 3, 4 and 5 – although most players carry only a 3 and 5 wood. The lower the number, the steeper the clubface and bigger the clubhead. Low numbers give you most distance; high numbers give you most height.

to clear any problems. A long iron is unlikely to give you a successful shot.

PLAYING THE SHOT

Grip the club normally and stand with the ball opposite the inside of your left heel. Aim the clubface square to the target and align your body parallel to the ball-to-target line. Make sure that the sole of the clubhead rests flat on the ground at address.

Because of the long shaft, your posture is more upright than normal. This creates a flat swing plane. Take the club away slowly, keeping a smooth tempo during the entire swing. The clubface sweeps the ball cleanly off the turf without taking a divot.

Remember you don't have to increase the speed of your swing to find extra distance. Power and clubhead speed are created by the long shaft, which in turn produces a wider arc.

Do's and don'ts
- DO use a 2, 3, 4 or 5 wood for distance from fairway or rough, and for height to clear an obstacle.
- DO check that the ball is opposite the inside of your left heel, and further away from your feet than for an iron to allow for the longer shaft.
- DO keep an even tempo.
- DON'T increase the speed of your swing.
- DON'T use a driver from the fairway.
- DON'T take a gamble – in a tricky lie choose your most lofted wood.

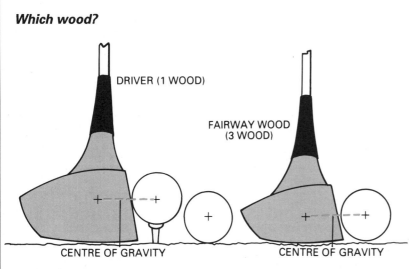

Which wood?

DRIVER (1 WOOD)

FAIRWAY WOOD (3 WOOD)

CENTRE OF GRAVITY   CENTRE OF GRAVITY

It's difficult to achieve height when the clubhead's centre of gravity is above the middle of the ball at impact. A driver has a high centre of gravity and is designed for striking a ball off a tee peg.

With a fairway wood most of the weight is near the bottom of the clubhead. It strikes below the centre of a ball on the ground, propelling it upwards without sacrificing distance.

Long iron approach

F ear strikes deep into the hearts of far too many golfers as they set up for a long iron to a green. But there's no need to be nervous. Though an approach with a long iron is more difficult than with a short iron, it's only slightly more so.

Negative thoughts affect your technique, so wayward or mis-struck long irons are usually a result of a poor mental state. Expecting a poor shot before you play is bound to hinder the stroke.

Often, negative thinkers take little care over their set-up and aim because they are used to trusting to luck rather than their method.

Most also change their swing. They seem to have an inbuilt mechanism that makes them hit the ball harder, believing that the further you have to hit it, the faster you must swing. This combinations of a sloppy set-up and rapid rhythm can only lead to disaster.

To produce consistently good results, you must unite a positive attitude with sound basics and a smooth, even tempo. Let the club do the work – a long iron is designed to hit the ball further than a short iron so you don't have to force the shot.

SET SQUARE

Take time to aim and set up properly. Set your blade square to the target and then move your body in to position. Make sure you're aligned perfectly parallel to the ball to target line, and the ball is placed correctly just inside your left heel.

For the best chance of returning the blade square at impact a solid set-up and a controlled, rhythmical swing are essential. A square

LONG SUFFERING
There is no need to be afraid to hit a long iron – remember that the difference in technique between playing a 7 iron and a 2 iron is very small. The only changes are the ball position – slightly more forward for a long iron – and a fractionally wider stance. If you realize this – so that your swing stays the same – and think positively, the ball should sear at the flag from long distance.

LONG RANGE ATTACK

1 CRUCIAL ADDRESS

A sound set-up is critical for long iron success, as any mistake is accentuated with a straighter faced club. Make sure you align perfectly parallel to the target line and the ball is placed correctly. It's also vital for your blade to be set square to the target. Your posture should be relaxed but not sloppy.

2 ON LINE TAKEAWAY

Be sure your takeaway is in one piece – don't just use your arms. At the full extent of the takeaway your shaft should be parallel to your feet and the ground. Taking the club back too far on the inside or the outside has a knock on effect and makes it hard to get the club back on plane for the downswing.

3 HALFWAY BACK

A good takeaway position should naturally lead your backswing into the correct plane. Halfway to the top, your shoulder turn should be already quite full. And if you're on perfect plane, the angle of your shaft to the ground should be the same as at address.

4 POINTING PARALLEL

Good moves on the backswing mean you can put the club in the correct position at the top of the backswing – pointing parallel to the target line and the ground. There should be no hint of overswing as this leads to getting ahead of the ball at impact.

5 CONTROLLED DOWN
The first move on the downswing is a pull down with the hands but the club should stay on plane even if the path is steeper than on the backswing. Keep the action smooth, rhythmical and controlled.

6 INTO IMPACT
If your backswing is good and the initial stages of the downswing on plane, your club should attack the ball from slightly inside the line, so the blade returns square at impact. Don't thrash at the ball – keep the swing simple and fluid.

7 FREELY THROUGH
Swing through freely, letting your hands release naturally after impact. A tell-tale sign of a correct down and through swing is if the angle of the shaft halfway to the finish position is the same as at address and halfway back.

8 BALANCED FINISH
Provided you have swung with an even tempo and kept the club on plane, your finish position should be balanced with your body facing the target. Your weight should be firmly on your left side.

Top draw

So often a handicap golfer struggles to reach a long distance target – particularly into wind – because they either play the wrong shot or choose the wrong club.

Because a 3 wood flies further than a 1 iron in normal conditions, it shouldn't be an automatic choice when shooting into a wind. The 3 wood can balloon and land short, but you can keep the long iron low and running by playing a draw.

It is possible to hit the draw with a wood, but because of it's design a long iron is easier to manipulate. Aim the blade square and align a fraction to the right. Swing normally – don't force the shot – let the combination of the closed stance and square blade do the work.

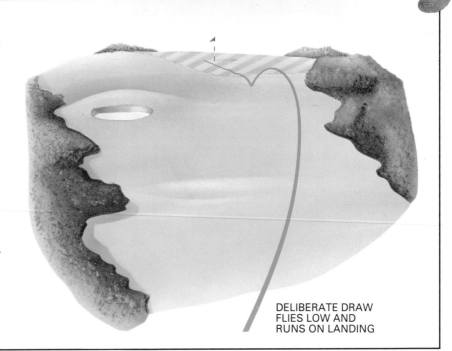

DELIBERATE DRAW
FLIES LOW AND
RUNS ON LANDING

clubface is critical to long iron success, as sidespin is accentuated by a straight faced club. The ball veers off line more than when you hit a short iron, because lofted clubs produce more backspin than sidespin.

LONG MANOEUVRES

Often you can gain an advantage if you shape a shot to a green – perhaps to land a ball softly or to avoid trouble. So the way a long iron is able to move the ball in the air can work in your favour.

Sometimes it's hard to stop a long iron on a green – especially if the ground is firm. But you can easily play a controlled fade that flies higher and has more backspin than normal by just changing your set-up slightly. With the blade still square, align a fraction to the left and swing as normal along the line of your feet.

It's also easy to draw the ball with a long iron, which is particularly useful when firing into a wind. You can hit a long raking runner that flies low and moves from right to left. The ball can go surprising distances, and is more likely to find the target than a high flying wood.

Too many golfers overlook long irons when practising. But if you're to be totally competent with all aspects of your play, you must work hard on them – never spurn long iron practice.

masterclass

Faldo's finale

Nick Faldo's confidence and prowess with the long irons have helped him win many championships. But one exacting strike thrilled thousands at Wentworth in 1989

In the 36 hole final of the World Matchplay, Nick reached the last hole and had never been in front. His opponent Ian Woosnam had set the pace and played scintillating golf throughout the final. But Faldo had all but matched him.

The double Open Champion played from the 28th to the 35th in 5 under to claw his way back to all square standing on the last tee.

After a perfectly positioned drive on the 502yd (459m) par 5, Faldo unleashed a 1 iron that drilled straight at the flag. It rolled past the pin and finished about 20ft (6m) behind the hole. After Woosie failed with an eagle putt from over 30ft (9m), Nick rolled his in for an incredible victory.

Faldo showed everyone watching exactly how a long iron to a green should be played. There seemed to be no strain involved at all. With a solid set-up and an even tempo swing, Nick had faith that the club would do what it was designed for.

Play the draw

The draw is a shot which starts to the right of the target and moves left in flight back towards the target. It's a useful shot for playing around a hazard. It also increases the distance of your shot because the ball rolls on landing more than it does for a straight shot or a fade. This makes it an ef-fective shot to play with woods and long irons.

The draw is a feel shot so it's not easy. Persevere with it and it will give great flexibility to your game.

When playing the draw, the first principle to understand is precisely how the ball spins from right to left in the air.

If you have a table tennis bat handy, try spinning a ping pong ball from right to left across a table. You soon realize that you need to brush the bat across the ball from *left* to *right* to achieve the spin you want.

Playing a draw in golf is exactly

THE ADVANTAGES OF A DRAW
The draw shot is a great asset when you want to hit the ball around a hazard or a tree. Also play a draw to increase your distance – the ball rolls further on landing.

Aim and align right

IN-TO-OUT SWING PATH

RIGHT FOOT BACK – STANCE SLIGHTLY CLOSED

Aim the club right of the target to allow for the draw spin and to help you visualize an in-to-out swing path. Align your body right of the ball-to-target line, by bringing your right foot back slightly.

FEEL THE SHOT

The draw is a feel shot. To improve your feeling for the in-to-out swing path required imagine you're standing in the centre of a clockface. The ball is positioned exactly in the middle and your ball-to-target line stretches from 6 o'clock to 12 o'clock. Now feel as if you're swinging to 7 o'clock on your backswing and to 1 o'clock on your throughswing.

When you hit the draw shot your swing automatically becomes slightly flatter on the backswing.

This is because your club is swinging more to the inside. On the throughswing, your left arm is more extended than normal as the club swings outside the ball-to-target line. The ball-to-target line remains the same as usual.

the same. You produce an in-to-out swing path, which takes the clubhead inside the ball-to-target line and then outside it after impact. The clubhead brushes left to right through the ball, like the table tennis bat.

AIM AND ALIGNMENT

Aim the clubface slightly to the right of the ball-to-target line. This helps you to visualize the in-to-out swing path and also allows for the draw spin. Now align your body parallel to the clubface, by bringing your right foot back a little.

Your body should now be aligned just to the right of target. Correct aim and alignment are essential if you are to start the ball to the right.

Because the draw is a feel shot, first try it with a club you're comfortable with – a 6 or 7 iron. As your confidence grows, move on to the more difficult longer clubs.

masterclass

Tom Watson's winning draw

Many of the world's top players use the draw to give them extra control. Tom Watson, who dominated world golf in the late 70s and early 80s, plays a draw as an important part of his game.

Watson has won the US Masters on two occasions, 1977 and 1981. He can thank his draw for these successes, because Augusta is laid out to suit players who have mastered the draw. It's no coincidence that Lee Trevino, the greatest player of the fade, has never triumphed at Augusta.

A well-played draw is a penetrating shot. This makes it a handy shot for windy courses, where you can fight or use a strong wind to your advantage. Watson's record on the windy, links courses of the Open Championship proves the point. He has won five times.

How to fade

When you hit a fade shot, the ball is struck left of the target but travels right during flight. Your most likely use for it is when there is an obstacle such as a large tree between you and your target.

The fade is an advanced, controlled shot – unlike the slice, a poor hit that also moves the ball from left to right during flight.

You achieve the fade by changing your body alignment at address. This alters your swing path – not the swing itself – and puts sidespin on the ball.

The ball flies higher and runs shorter than a normal shot. You may have to take a slightly less lofted club than usual (for instance, a 5 iron instead of a 6 iron).

ALIGN LEFT OF TARGET

Your body should align left of the ball-to-target line, while you keep the clubface aimed square on to it. Slightly open your hips and shoulders by turning them left and swing normally. Your swing follows an out-to-in path: the clubhead travels from right to left across the standard swing path, causing it to brush through the ball and giving it sidespin. There is no need to change your grip.

You must have confidence in your set-up and your swing to achieve a successful fade, so rehearse the shot on the practice range. It is a 'feel' shot – you must be able to see the shot in your mind if you are to play it well.

Once you have developed a consistent routine, you are ready to attempt the shot on the course.

WHAT HAPPENS WHEN YOU FADE

Fade swing path (out to in)
By aligning your body left of the ball-to-target line, in an open position, you automatically shift your swing path. Compared with a normal swing path, the fade produces a path that travels outside the normal line on the backswing and downswing, but moves inside that same line on the throughswing. You alter only your address position to achieve a fade. You do not change your swing to change your swing path.

Clock golf
To help you see your fade swing path in your mind, imagine you are teed up on the centre of a clockface, facing 3 o'clock. When you hit a straight shot, you hit along a ball-to-target line stretching from 6 o'clock to 12 o'clock. When you fade correctly, that ball-to-target line remains the same – but you in fact hit along a line from 5 o'clock to 11 o'clock.

FADE SWING PATH

NORMAL SWING PATH

OPEN STANCE

BALL-TO-TARGET LINE

Path of ball
The fade shot is ideal for playing around obstacles such as a row of trees. A faded ball starts out on a line which is left of the intended target. During its flight the spinning ball returns to a more central position by moving right in the air.

CHANGING YOUR SWING PATH

NORMAL TAKEAWAY

FADE TAKEAWAY

NORMAL SET-UP
In normal set-up, your feet, hips and shoulders are parallel to the imaginary ball-to-target line. During normal takeaway and backswing, the club travels on a straight path inside and parallel to the ball-to-target line. Throughout the swing, the club remains inside this line.

FADE SET-UP
Move your left foot about 6in (15cm) away from the club closest to your feet. This aligns you left of target. Keep the clubface square to the ball-to-target line, even if this imaginary line passes through the obstacle. Although you swing normally, adjustment at address produces an out-to-in swing path, which gives sidespin.

masterclass

Nicklaus' percentage fade
At the 18th tee at Augusta, Nicklaus fades the ball around the right-hand dog-leg, avoiding the bunker on the left. The ball is shown in mid-air, just about to drop.

Nicklaus also uses the fade to reduce his margin for error in a straight shot. Imagine you are 160yd (145m) from the green with a centrally positioned flag and 30ft (9m) either side. If you aim straight at the flag but slice it 20ft (6m) wide, you have a long putt.

Nicklaus' tactic is to aim the shot 10ft (3m) left of the pin and fade the ball. Should he over-fade it by 20ft (6m), he is only 10ft (3m) right of the pin. Should he hit it straight by mistake he is still only 10ft (3m) from the hole, this time on the left. If he hits well he is closer still.

Tackling sloping approaches

Far too many golfers become frustrated and nervous when they have to play a shot from a sloping lie. Negative thoughts take over – even if the target is a short iron away – and trusting to luck becomes the order of the day.

This lack of confidence stems from a hazy knowledge of the techniques needed to pull off an approach from a slope. An understanding of the different set-ups for the various lies is essential to your success.

FLIGHT PLAN

For every shot you face from a slope – it could be an uphill, downhill, sidehill or combination lie – you must also know the shape of flight that's produced.

The flight varies markedly – low and slightly left to right from a downhill lie, or turning right to left when the ball is above your feet. Working out the flight path and setting up to compensate for it are the keys to accurate approaches.

A blend of a subtly changed set-up and technique isn't enough – club selection is critical. Because the flights vary so much, you have to hit a different club from your normal choice for a certain distance. From the same yardage, the club you hit can vary by as much as four depending on the type and severity of slope.

On a steep downslope you can sometimes hit as little as a 9 iron even from a distance of 150yd (137m). But from an upslope you could play a 5 iron for the same length.

Finally, after taking time to plan your shot, play the stroke with authority. Have the conviction that your preparations and a smooth, balanced swing send the ball searing at the flag.

BANK MANAGER
A balanced and stable stance gives you the base to tackle awkward sloping lies. Combined with simple alignment and aim changes and an easy rhythm, your body positioning holds the key to success. With the ball below your feet, it's critical to stay still when firing into a green – a smooth swing with a steady head and body guards against the thin.

BEAT THE SLOPES

DOWNHILL

From a downslope the ball flies low, slightly left to right and runs on landing. The steeper the slope and the longer the distance, the more the ball curves. Because of this flight, choose less club than the yardage suggests and aim left of the target. Put more weight than usual on your left side to move with the slope, and position the ball back in your stance. Both these moves ensure you strike the ball before the ground yet guard against the thin.

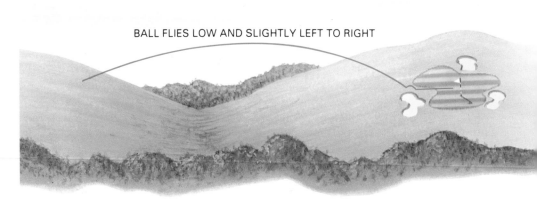

BALL FLIES LOW AND SLIGHTLY LEFT TO RIGHT

UPSLOPE

The ball flies high and slightly right to left and stops quickly from an uphill lie. To compensate for this flight take more club than the yardage suggests and align and aim right of target. Your weight should favour your right side to counter the slope. Position the ball forward in your stance. This set-up helps you to swing along the slope and catch the ball crisply. If the ball's too far back you strike down and can stab the shot.

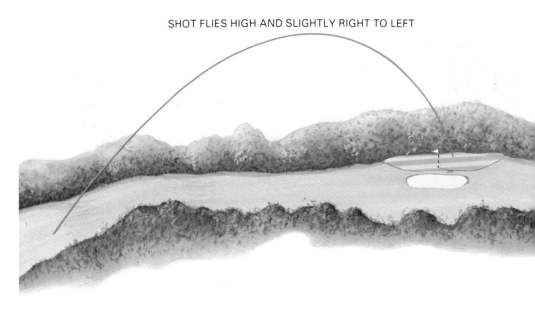

SHOT FLIES HIGH AND SLIGHTLY RIGHT TO LEFT

SIDEHILL – BALL BELOW FEET

As your plane naturally becomes more upright than normal when the ball is below your feet, the shot flies from left to right. You must align and aim left of target to compensate for this fading flight. When the slope is quite severe aim well left of your target – especially as the ball kicks right on landing. Because the ball fades you have to take more club than the yardage suggests. You may find that you have to stoop a little more than usual to reach the ball, but try not to become too crouched. Gripping at the end of the club helps keep your posture as normal as possible.

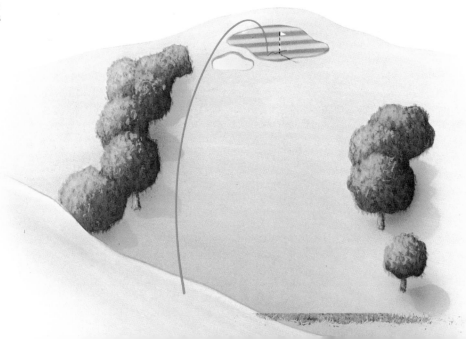

BALL MOVES FROM LEFT TO RIGHT AND KICKS RIGHT ON LANDING

1 LEAN WITH THE SLOPE
Position the ball back in the stance and move your weight on to your left side to help a balanced swing.

2 SHORT TO THE TOP
Keep your backswing short so you don't overbalance. As you swing down resist moving your weight back on to the right side – stay on the left.

3 FOLLOW THE LEVEL
Swing into and through impact keeping the club close to the level of the slope. This ensures against the thin or top and leads you into a slightly crouched throughswing position.

Distance: 140yd (128m)
Grip: normal
Stance: align and aim slightly left of target
Ball position: back in stance
Weight distribution: favour your left side
Swing: short of normal
Swing path: normal
Club: 9 iron

1 FORWARD PLACEMENT
Move the ball forward in your stance and position more weight than usual on your right side to encourage a sweeping strike.

2 STAY BALANCED
Follow the line of the slope into and through impact and resist moving your weight on to the left side too soon. This action helps you to strike the ball crisply and avoid the stab.

3 THROUGH CONTROL
Lead through the stroke with the left hand to lessen the draw on the ball, and move on to your left side for a balanced finish.

Distance: 140yd (128m)
Grip: normal
Stance: align and aim slightly right of target
Ball position: forward in stance
Weight distribution: favour your right side
Swing: short of normal
Swing path: normal
Club: 6 iron

1 COMFORTABLE ADDRESS
The key to this shot is to have a balanced and stable stance. Grip up the club and bend the knees to help you reach the ball. If it's well below your feet, try spreading your legs.

2 STEADY HEAD
It's very important to keep your head perfectly level and still throughout the backswing, to help stay balanced and improve your chances of swinging down on the correct path.

3 LEVEL ATTACK
Attack the ball with your head steady and the same amount of flex in the knees as at address. This helps you avoid rising up and coming off the shot. If you don't, a thin or top is likely.

Distance: 140yd (128m)
Grip: further up than normal
Stance: align and aim left of target
Ball position: normal
Weight distribution: normal
Swing: full
Swing path: slightly more upright than usual
Club: 6 iron

SHOT DRAWS AND KICKS LEFT ON LANDING

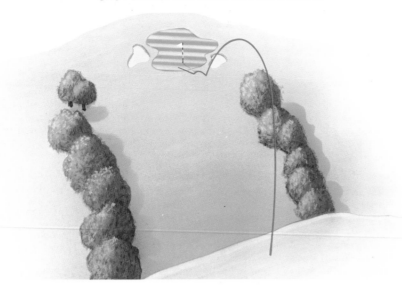

Choke down to help posture and control.

Distance: 140yd (128m)
Grip: choke down
Stance: align and aim right of target
Ball position: normal
Weight distribution: normal
Swing: full
Swing path: slightly flatter than usual
Club: 8 iron

BALL ABOVE FEET
When the ball is above your feet your swing naturally becomes flatter and the shot draws and runs to the left on landing. Because of this flight you have to aim well right of the target – especially off a steep slope – and take less club than the yardage suggests. It's important you judge the shot so that the ball pitches short and right of the target as the drawspin makes it difficult to stop the ball. Choke down the club to help keep your posture and swing as normal as possible.

Hill training

To bolster confidence of sloping approach shots, it's essential to practise them and gain an understanding of the techniques.

There is no real substitute for working on these shots outside on the range or on the course. When you can't find a suitable spot on the practice ground try to seek an alternative way to fine tune your skills.

Increasingly, slope trainers can be found at driving ranges and are a valuable aid. The platform moves hydraulically and you can set it to the slope and angle you prefer. A few sessions on the trainer should give you confidence to play accurate shots out on the course.

Practice becomes even more vital if you're to play on a links – especially if you usually play on a flat course. Links ground is dune ridden and even the fairways undulate severely in places.

Royal Birkdale is a classic example of links golf and almost all the fairways are lined with huge grassy sandhills. If you're not practised and proficient an encounter with a steep slope can lead to more trouble. Notice how US pro Rica Comstock stays perfectly balanced during the shot – something you must practise for slope success.

Control in the wind

PLAYING IN THE WIND
Assess the wind carefully and keep the ball low. If you're using an iron, play the shot with the ball slightly nearer your right foot than normal to deloft the clubface. Maintaining good tempo and rhythm is vital for playing well in the wind.

A shot struck perfectly into the wind should stay straight. But if you're a high handicapper, wind from any direction is likely to blow your ball off-line unless you adjust your technique. To play well in the wind you must understand the effect it has on the ball so you can reduce the damage.

Wind exaggerates spin. You have to strike cleanly because even a small miss-hit can be heavily penalized. For example, if you slice into a left-to-right wind the ball travels even further off-line than in normal conditions.

In windy weather you must prepare thoroughly for each shot

Grip down
Because you need as much control in the wind as possible, grip about 2in (5cm) further down the club than normal. The closer your hands are to the clubhead and the ball, the greater clubface feel you have through impact.

LEFT-TO-RIGHT WIND

Imagine a flag to the left of the real target and aim the clubface at that. Align your body parallel to this substitute ball-to-target line and let the wind blow the ball to the real pin.

RIGHT-TO-LEFT WIND

Aim the clubface and align your body right of the real flag. Because your upper body now faces away from the target this set-up feels strange but have confidence in your aim and don't rush your swing.

INTO THE WIND

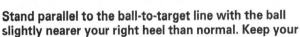

Stand parallel to the ball-to-target line with the ball slightly nearer your right heel than normal. Keep your head still through impact, making sure your tempo stays smooth and even.

DOWNWIND

You can make a smooth swing because the wind does the work for you. Beware of the bunkers and other obstacles you can't normally reach – they may be now in range.

or your game will be blown apart. You need to assess the wind's strength and direction, select the most suitable club for the stroke and make changes to your set-up and technique.

ASSESS THE WIND

The simplest way of assessing the strength and direction of the wind is to throw a few blades of grass into the air and notice how they are blown. Check how the flag on the green is flying – if you're in a sheltered position, see if the tops of the trees or bushes are moving and how strongly.

Whatever the direction of the wind, it's often a good idea to play the ball low. If the land is flat and the lie is good, try to run the ball along the ground for as long as possible. The higher you hit the ball the more it's affected by the wind. Wind currents are stronger higher up, and hedges, bushes and trees give shelter at ground level.

If the wind is against you, a low stroke travels further and straighter than a high shot because of the reduced wind resistance nearer the ground.

With a following wind, your ball is certain to fly further than usual. Make sure that hazards such as bunkers you can't normally reach are not now in range – if they are, club down to play safe and keep control.

CROSS WINDS

Make adjustments in your alignment to use the wind to your advantage. For example, with a right-to-left wind, aim your shot right of the target and let the ball move back towards the flag on the currents. How far left or right you aim depends on the wind's strength.

Because most players slice, a left-to-right wind causes extra problems for a right-hander. A left-

PLAY SAFE TO LIMIT SLICE

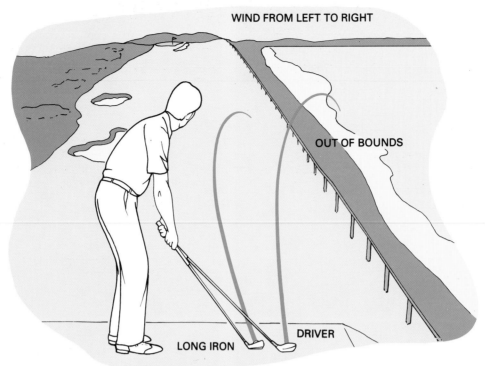

WIND FROM LEFT TO RIGHT

OUT OF BOUNDS

LONG IRON DRIVER

When a strong wind is blowing from the left and there is out of bounds on the right, take an iron off the tee for safety.

A slice is the most common fault in the game and a left-to-right wind exaggerates any clockwise spin on the ball, blowing it further to the right and into trouble.

Because an iron doesn't hit the ball as far as a wood – and is also easier to control – the ball is more likely to stay on course.

Accept that your next shot will be longer than usual – but at least you'll be hitting from the fairway, which gives you much more chance of keeping control.

Stay warm to concentrate
If the wind is very strong a woollen hat helps you concentrate on your game as well as keeping you warm. Pull the hat right over your ears to block out the cold and muffle distractions while you play a stroke.

hander finds wind blowing from the right more difficult.

HITTING THE SHOT

Take care over club selection. Depending on the strength of a wind that's against you, you may have to take up to three clubs more than normal to make up the distance.

Make sure you strike cleanly by reducing the length of your swing to three-quarter or even half – but again be guided by the wind's strength. Don't try to gain extra distance by hitting harder – it severely reduces your chances of playing a good shot.

If you decide to hit the ball low under the wind, you must make changes to your set-up and swing. Grip the club about 2in (5cm) further down the shaft than usual to increase your control and feel of the clubface.

Take up a slightly narrower stance than normal. This automatically reduces the length and power of your swing and helps you to make a clean strike. Stay calm and think positive before you start

your swing.

There's no need to change your regular ball position when using a wood. But with an iron place the ball slightly nearer your right foot than usual. This ensures impact is on the downstroke which lessens the loft and keeps the ball low. Keep your head still through impact and concentrate on shifting your weight to your left side as you swing through.

MENTAL APPROACH

Try to keep good tempo and rhythm at all times. Because the game is more difficult in the wind and scores get higher, many golfers increase the speed of their swing in a vain attempt to hit the ball harder and further. This only makes matters worse. You must keep a cool head and accept that your total will be higher than average.

Concentrate on making a smooth swing and have confidence in your game plan. Take your time when selecting your club and don't rush your set-up and stroke.

Using the wind

Get the wind to help you lower your scores – use it rather than fight it. If you are confident in your approach, you can turn both tail-winds and headwinds to your advantage.

A tailwind can help you increase your distance and improve your tempo, and a headwind can help you stop your ball quickly on the green.

Playing these positive shots brings greater confidence to your all-round play.

USING A TAILWIND

The key to playing downwind is to concentrate on keeping a smooth rhythm and staying relaxed – the same as in other wind situations.

Do not let the wind disturb your timing. Your club and the wind combine to do the work for you, and your ball soars further down the fairway than usual.

When you stand on the tee with the wind behind you, consider the options, as a tailwind has more uses than simply gaining extra distance.

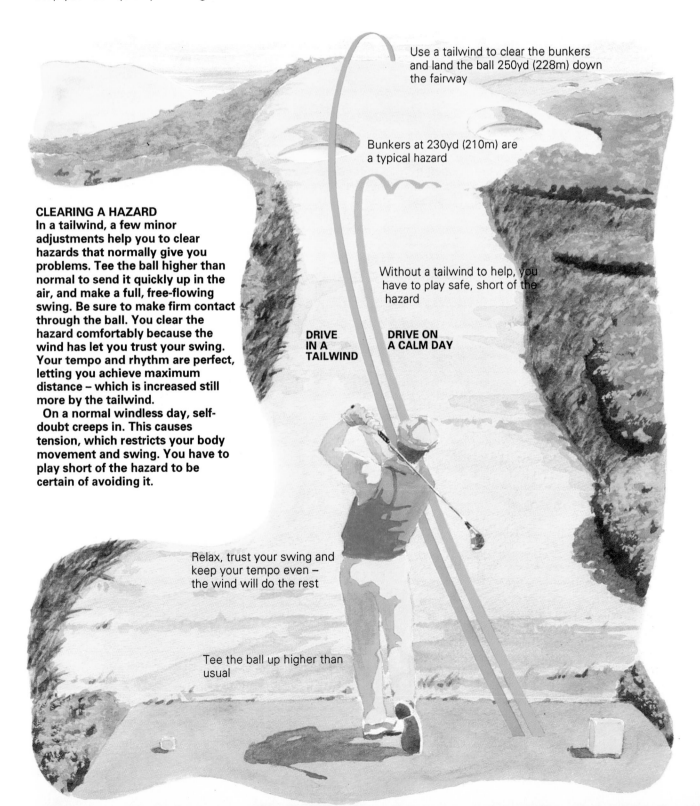

CLEARING A HAZARD
In a tailwind, a few minor adjustments help you to clear hazards that normally give you problems. Tee the ball higher than normal to send it quickly up in the air, and make a full, free-flowing swing. Be sure to make firm contact through the ball. You clear the hazard comfortably because the wind has let you trust your swing. Your tempo and rhythm are perfect, letting you achieve maximum distance – which is increased still more by the tailwind.

On a normal windless day, self-doubt creeps in. This causes tension, which restricts your body movement and swing. You have to play short of the hazard to be certain of avoiding it.

Use a tailwind to clear the bunkers and land the ball 250yd (228m) down the fairway

Bunkers at 230yd (210m) are a typical hazard

Without a tailwind to help, you have to play safe, short of the hazard

DRIVE IN A TAILWIND

DRIVE ON A CALM DAY

Relax, trust your swing and keep your tempo even – the wind will do the rest

Tee the ball up higher than usual

Play safe without losing distance

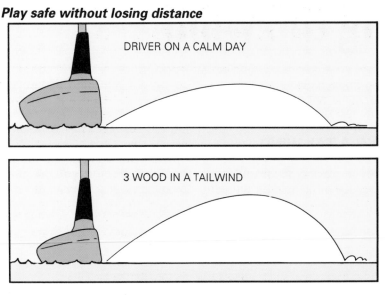

DRIVER ON A CALM DAY

3 WOOD IN A TAILWIND

If you are nervous with your driver, a 3 wood hit with no extra effort in a tailwind gives you as much distance as a driver would on a windless day.

Your more composed attitude helps you to swing correctly and keep your rhythm. The greater loft of the 3 wood sends the ball up and it is then taken by the wind.

A huge drive can make your second shot easier, but it can also send your ball into the trees or out of bounds. If you want to play safe, and do not feel confident with your driver, club down to a 3 wood.

Tee the ball higher than normal and set up with your weight slightly favouring (about 60% of your body weight) your right side. Although you make a full swing, your set-up ensures that you hit the ball on the upswing. The ball should rise quickly into the air and be taken by the wind.

The ball travels just as far as it does with a full drive in windless conditions. You also have the ad-vantage of more ball control because the extra loft of the 3 wood makes your shot easier to play, increasing your confidence.

USING A HEADWIND

A headwind is a huge asset in stop-ping your ball quickly on the green, which lets you fire your ball straight at the pin.

You must be confident and keep your rhythm. Trust your swing to take care of the shot. Don't let the wind in your face disturb your concentration by causing you to swing more quickly than normal.

Whatever the distance is to the green, take more club than normal (for example, a 7 iron when you would normally use a 9 iron) and be sure to make a firm hit. Do not be afraid of overshooting the green with the extra club – the strong headwind causes the ball to hang in the air longer than you expect before it falls softly to the green.

As you strike through the ball, make a positive weight shift to your left side into a balanced followthrough position.

Using headwind to stop your ball

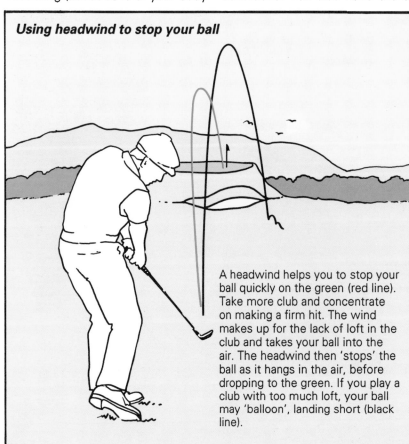

A headwind helps you to stop your ball quickly on the green (red line). Take more club and concentrate on making a firm hit. The wind makes up for the lack of loft in the club and takes your ball into the air. The headwind then 'stops' the ball as it hangs in the air, before dropping to the green. If you play a club with too much loft, your ball may 'balloon', landing short (black line).

masterclass

Woosnam in the wind
Ian Woosnam is one of the shortest players in the world – and also one of the longest hitters. The stocky Welshman is perfectly comfortable in the wind because he concentrates on weight transfer to give good balance. He gains maximum roll on his long shots by using the wind to favour his natural draw as much as possible.

Choke down for control

The best and safest way to keep the ball under control – especially in a wind – is to grip down the club a little and use a shorter swing than normal.

Choking down naturally shortens the swing arc – you stand closer to the ball so you feel compact which leads to greater confidence. Your wrists also become stiffer, helping to keep the ball lower than usual.

TACKLING THE WIND

Because you hit the ball low, the grip down shot is mainly used for playing in a wind. Most amateur golfers think of choking down only when firing into the wind, but it also has crucial uses in both a cross and downwind.

If you hit your usual club for the distance in a **headwind** the shot towers and falls well short of the target. Take more club – up to four clubs in a strong wind – and grip down. Play the ball from further back in your stance. This produces much backspin and gives you greater control.

With your hands pushed ahead of the ball, make a three-quarter swing. Keep your hands ahead of the ball at impact and finish short. The ball flies low, boring through the wind, but still lands softly as it's held on the air.

When you're on the fairway and face a shot of 3 wood distance into wind it's sometimes best to hit a choked down driver with a shorter swing. The ball stays low and under the wind and reaches the target – a 3 wood climbs too high and falls short.

In a **crosswind** you can use the same iron technique. The ball doesn't drift as far on the wind as a normal stroke – this is most useful if there's trouble around the green. But you do have to aim either slightly to the left or right of the target – depending on the direction of the wind – as the ball still drifts a little.

If you feel confident, try to hold the ball on the crosswind. Use a faint draw into a left to right wind, or a soft fade into a breeze coming in from the right.

Downwind, too, the choke down shot has its advantages. When faced with an awkward length pitch – when you can't hit a full shot that stops – you have to play a pitch and run.

Instead of hitting a wedge you should play a straighter faced club – perhaps an 8 iron. Grip down and use a firm wristed, half shot action. The ball flies low and pitches well short of the target but runs on landing.

It's surprising how much control and finesse you can apply when you play this shot. The type of action is also very useful for playing

SECURITY SHOT
Learning the skills to play the choke down shot – and knowing you can pull it off with ease – gives you a great feeling of security. You needn't be worried by a left to right wind – even if there's trouble on the right. An easy rhythm punch shot under the wind – with a 7 iron from about 125yd (115m), for example – has a much better chance of going close to the target than a normal high flyer.

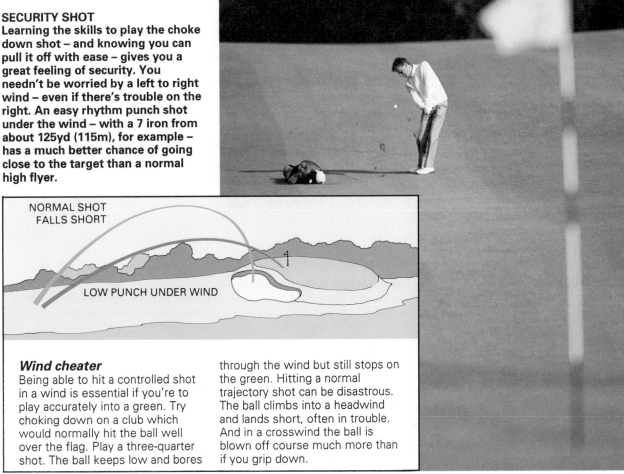

NORMAL SHOT FALLS SHORT

LOW PUNCH UNDER WIND

Wind cheater
Being able to hit a controlled shot in a wind is essential if you're to play accurately into a green. Try choking down on a club which would normally hit the ball well over the flag. Play a three-quarter shot. The ball keeps low and bores through the wind but still stops on the green. Hitting a normal trajectory shot can be disastrous. The ball climbs into a headwind and lands short, often in trouble. And in a crosswind the ball is blown off course much more than if you grip down.

CONTROLLED PUNCH

BACK IN THE STANCE/SHORT AT THE TOP
Choose more club than the yardage suggests. Align parallel to the ball-to-target line and position the ball just inside your right heel. Choke down the club and square up the blade. Your hands must be ahead of the ball. With a smooth unhurried action and little wrist break take the club back on a wide path. Move up into a three-quarter length backswing position and turn fully.

HANDS AHEAD AT IMPACT/STOP SHORT
Swing down smoothly and lead the stroke with your left hand. Keep your hands ahead of the clubface through impact to ensure the ball flies low. Concentrate on striking the ball before the ground. Swing through into a short yet balanced finish. This is natural if you extend fully through the ball on a wide arc – the ball climbs too high if you release the hands.

delicate chips round the green – the more you go down the grip the easier it is to control the clubhead and the more your touch is refined.

The choke down shot is a valuable asset when recovering **from trouble**. Often after driving into trees you have to play a low shot **out under branches**. Going down the grip on a long iron lets you keep the ball low and – most importantly – under control.

You can also choke down when the **ball is above your feet**. This helps you adopt a balanced stance and use your normal swing, and reduces the often damaging drawspin.

When playing from a **fairway bunker** it's easier to strike the ball cleanly with the stiffer wristed and shorter swing of a choked down shot. This is essential when you must play safe, and an escape from the trap is the priority. Hitting a normal shot increases the risk of either thinning or fatting the stroke.

masterclass

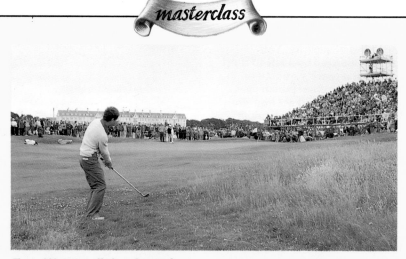

Tom Watson: links champion
The amiable American, one of the all time greats, has an unsurpassed record at the Open Championship in modern day golf. Watson's control and shotmaking ability on links courses are amazing – and the way he manipulates the ball in the wind is one key to his success.

A links course like Turnberry needs subtle and delicate handling as well as power. Watson has shown over the years that his touch approaching the greens is excellent. The choked down pitch and run from close in is a valuable weapon in Tom's armoury. Brilliant control helped him win five Open titles, three other top ten finishes and the Championship scoring record of 268 at Turnberry in 1977.

Driver off the fairway

The driver off the fairway is an extremely effective weapon when used in the correct way. But it should only be played when you can gain a definite advantage.

The shot produces a low-boring trajectory – ideal when hitting into wind, or for a long running ball to a distant target – but it's also difficult to play perfectly. Only advanced players should attempt this shot – it's not for high handicappers.

WEIGH UP THE RISKS

Use the shot to reach a long par 4 into the wind or to get home in 2 on a par 5. Yet if there is only a small chance of success and trouble looms near the green, it's wiser to play a long iron and then

THOUGHT AND TEMPO
The secret of success is positive and careful thinking, while maintaining good rhythm with a normal swing. With the feet slightly open the ball starts fractionally left and slides back to the right during flight. The ball flies low and can run long distances, perfect for playing into wind.

hit a short iron in.

The lie must be flat or slightly uphill – to act as a launching pad – and the ball must be sitting well, preferably on dry ground. When the ball is lying badly always think hard about hitting the shot even if there is a chance of reaching the green. It's a tricky enough shot to play well without added problems.

Many regard the driver off the fairway as the hardest of all shots, but as long as the lie is good the risks are mainly in the mind.

The fact that most good golfers happily hit a 3 wood off the fairway makes their fear all the more unnecessary.

There is only a slight difference in the degree of loft, the centre of gravity and length of shaft from a 3 wood to a driver. The driver is just a bit more difficult to play.

THE TECHNIQUE

The basic technique of hitting the driver from the fairway is the same as from a tee peg. At address, position the ball opposite or slightly in front of your left heel and aim the clubface at the target as normal.

Your feet should be fractionally open – this slightly increases the loft on the driver to help get the ball airborne and to guard against the snap hook. Because you are aligning slightly left and your clubface is square, the ball starts left and moves gently to the right in the flight.

Think positively – imagine you are hitting a 3 wood – and swing as normal. Don't overhit the ball – rhythm is far more important when applying power.

The key difference between hitting off the fairway and from a tee peg is timing. It needs to be spot on to achieve good results from the fairway. It's important to strike the ball at the bottom of your swing arc, and to sweep it off the turf.

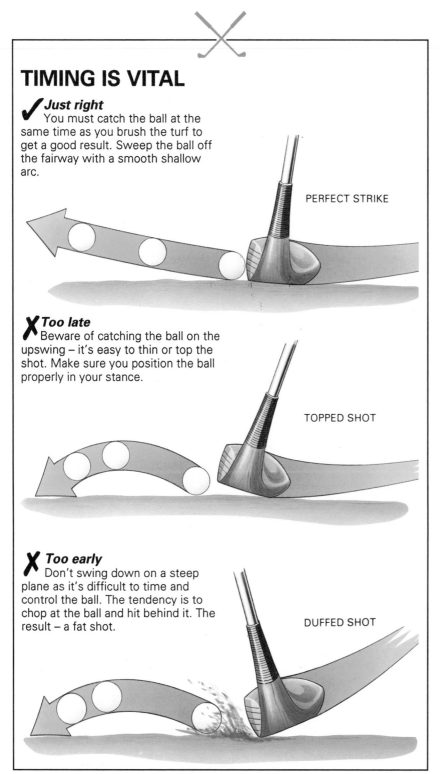

TIMING IS VITAL

✓ **Just right**
You must catch the ball at the same time as you brush the turf to get a good result. Sweep the ball off the fairway with a smooth shallow arc.

PERFECT STRIKE

✗ **Too late**
Beware of catching the ball on the upswing – it's easy to thin or top the shot. Make sure you position the ball properly in your stance.

TOPPED SHOT

✗ **Too early**
Don't swing down on a steep plane as it's difficult to time and control the ball. The tendency is to chop at the ball and hit behind it. The result – a fat shot.

DUFFED SHOT

masterclass

Ian's killer blow
The driver from the fairway presents Ian Woosnam with few problems because he is such a great timer of the ball. Combined with his power he can reach greens that are out of range for most golfers.

In the 1989 Irish Open at Portmarnock, the little Welshman came to the 514yd par-5 16th neck and neck with Philip Walton. But Woosie struck two drivers one after the other – the second off the fairway – to within 15ft (5m) of the hole to make birdie. He went on to win the title.

Low under the trees

Every golfer – no matter how good – ends up in trouble at some time, often among trees. What most amateurs see as a no hope situation can be turned into a positive result. Instead of chipping out sideways or bunting the ball only slightly further up the fairway, it's possible to play an attacking shot at the green.

Being able to hit the low drilling shot – often bending round trouble as well – is a valuable addition to your list of recovery shots.

The technique for hitting the low shot differs from a normal stroke in both set-up and swing, but the changes are simple. The ball is further back in the stance, the swing shorter and with less wrist break. But the most vital difference is in your club selection.

To keep the ball low you must use a straight faced iron – anything above a 7 iron climbs too high off the clubface and can easily tangle in the branches. If you use a 6 iron for a normal shot of 165yd (150m), you probably need either a 3 or 4 iron to hit a low shot under trees the same distance.

WHICH SHOT?

The club you choose also depends on what shape of shot you have to hit. If you need to play a deliberate hook or draw as well as keeping the ball low, a 6 iron might be enough to reach the green. Your changed set-up naturally takes loft off the clubface and makes it play like a 4 iron. The ball also runs on landing as the draw spin gains extra yardage.

When you cut the ball low and left to right, you must take more club than the yardage suggests. To play this shot you have to open up the blade – increasing its loft – so that a 5 iron becomes like a 7. The 5 then runs the risk of crashing into the branches. You must play a straighter faced club – perhaps even a 1 iron if you need to hit the ball a long way.

PUNCHING POWER
Too many golfers try to hit a full shot out under trees, with disastrous results – the ball crashes into the branches. A simple change in set-up and swing means you play an attacking and controlled long punch shot at the green.

RUNNING LOW

1 ADDRESS
For the low running fade, aim your clubface at the target and align left. Position the ball back in your stance. Grip down the club slightly for better control, and push your hands forward. For the straight shot only your alignment should alter – you must stand parallel to the ball-to-target line. Align right to draw the ball.

2 SHORT CONTROLLED BACKSWING
Your swing should be exactly the same whether you are playing a low fade, draw or straight shot. Take the club away on a shallow path with little wrist break. The backswing should be three-quarter length, and your left arm almost straight. You must still make a full shoulder turn.

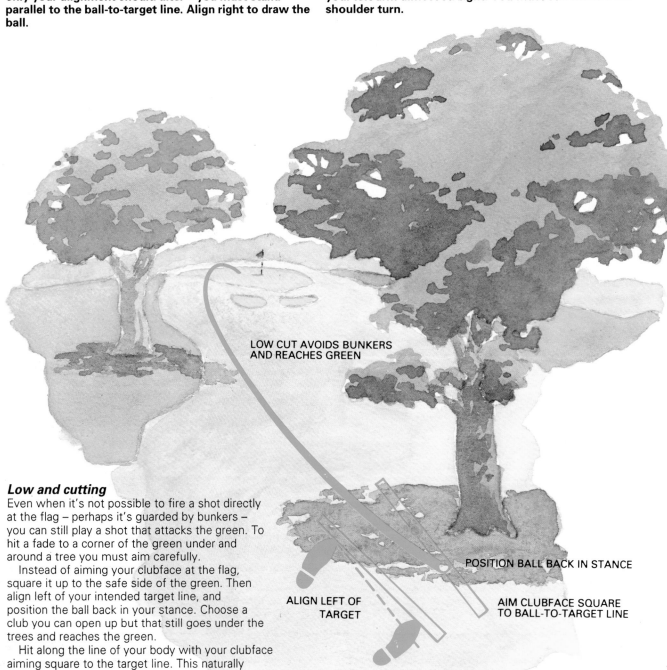

LOW CUT AVOIDS BUNKERS
AND REACHES GREEN

POSITION BALL BACK IN STANCE

ALIGN LEFT OF
TARGET

AIM CLUBFACE SQUARE
TO BALL-TO-TARGET LINE

Low and cutting
Even when it's not possible to fire a shot directly at the flag – perhaps it's guarded by bunkers – you can still play a shot that attacks the green. To hit a fade to a corner of the green under and around a tree you must aim carefully.

Instead of aiming your clubface at the flag, square it up to the safe side of the green. Then align left of your intended target line, and position the ball back in your stance. Choose a club you can open up but that still goes under the trees and reaches the green.

Hit along the line of your body with your clubface aiming square to the target line. This naturally shapes the shot from left to right – if you play it precisely the ball should end up on the green.

3 DOWN TO IMPACT
Swing down with a smooth unhurried action – the harder you swing down the higher the ball flies which is dangerous. The combination of a sweeping downswing and the ball position makes for a crisp strike and the ball flies low. The ball starts left of target when you hit the fade.

4 EXTEND THROUGH AND STOP SHORT
Your extension through the ball should be as full as possible and your finish should be short – ensuring the ball drills low. But make sure you don't stop your followthrough too short as this leads to a stabbed shot. The combination of your alignment and aim sends the ball moving from left to right.

LOW DELIBERATE
DRAW ATTACKS FLAG

POSITION BALL BACK IN STANCE

IGN RIGHT OF TARGET

AIM CLUBFACE SQUARE
TO BALL-TO-TARGET LINE

Low and hooking
The normal draw around trees is simple to play, but having to go underneath branches as well needs a more precise execution. Select your club carefully. Look for one that can reach the green and keep low to go under branches but is lofted enough to fly a good distance and not snap hook and dribble along the ground.

Aim your club at the target but align your feet, hips and shoulders to the right – how much depends on how far you have to move the ball from right to left. Position the ball slightly further back than normal to help keep the ball low.

Your swing should be the same as for a straight low shot – the combination of your alignment and aim sends the ball curling right to left.

Use some ingenuity

A good imagination is essential for tackling tricky situations. When faced with a problem shot think through all possible options and try to be creative – there may be five or six strokes you could play. Trees give great scope for invention when there is some room to manoeuvre.

If you have to negotiate a series of trees, it may be possible to keep the ball low under all the branches, but reaching the green could be difficult. The stock option of hitting a low cutting shot round the second tree is on, but flirting with the greenside bunker is a danger.

A more imaginative shot – such as a cut up under the first tree but over the second that lands quite softly – could be the best choice. To play this shot you need a good understanding of technique, but above all trust in your own ability.

Confidence and conviction come from experimenting with various shots. The practice ground is the perfect arena for developing your imagination, but never be afraid to attempt the unusual at any time. Playing the creative shot bolsters your golf and adds to your enjoyment.

THOUGHTFUL ATTACK

One of the keys to playing this stroke well is good visualization.

Combine your thoughts on the shape of shot and clubbing with a keen awareness of the weather and state of the ground – bearing in mind that a low shot always runs on landing whatever the conditions. A low draw should usually run more than a fade – the ball has topspin on it as well as sidespin.

Your lie and other hazards between you and the green also affect your choice of shot.

Even if there are bunkers in front of the green and the flag is guarded by sand, you may be able to hit an attacking shot. There may be a way of avoiding the traps yet still reaching a corner of the green with deadly accurate aim.

But don't be over ambitious. Unless you have a realistic chance it's probably best to lay up short of the trouble and hope to pitch and putt.

King James conquers the Dukes

The Dukes Course at Woburn – home of the Dunhill British Masters – is completely treelined, which causes many golfers severe problems. But in 1990 England's Mark James negotiated the woods brilliantly to win with an 18 under par total.

His feat wasn't without a scare. At the 16th on the last day – only 2 strokes ahead of his nearest rival – his drive finished close to the large pine at the corner of the dog-leg, blocking him out from the green.

Using superb technique and imagination he created a low drawing 5 iron under and round the tree on to the green. He salvaged his par and held on over the final holes to beat David Feherty.

Positive rough play

Taking the safe option of playing a short iron back on to the fairway from rough, rather than going for the green, is usually wise. But with their sound technique most advanced players can usually play in a positive way even from thick rough. It sometimes pays to be brave so long as you're not over ambitious.

You must balance a positive attitude with careful thought. Learn when you can go for the green, and when you must play safe. If you desperately need birdies or have to reach the green for a chance to save the hole in matchplay, it's a good idea to be positive and take on the adventurous shot.

If trouble looms near the green or you have to clear bunkers or water, think again. The penalties for a bad shot are severe and outweigh the advantage gained if the shot comes off. But by using the correct technique it is still possible to play a positive stroke even if there is some trouble near the green.

FROM LIGHT ROUGH

The only changes you make to conventional technique are to attack the ball from a steeper angle and to play it from slightly further back in your stance. Your aim and alignment should stay the same as normal.

Be aware that the ball runs further from rough than from the fairway because of lack of backspin. Choose less club than normal to gain the same distance – perhaps an 8 iron instead of a 7.

STEEP ATTACK
A slight change in your technique can turn defensive play into positive when tackling a shot from rough grass. If you attack the ball with a steep downswing – by breaking your wrists early on the backswing – there is less grass between the clubface and the ball than with a normal stroke. This helps you to gain some control over the shot – you can go for the flag instead of playing safe.

The action of hitting down on the ball gains height on the shot. This means you can still go for the flag even if there's a bunker in the way – providing the distance between the trap and the hole is large enough.

From long range it's often a good idea to hit a smooth, sweeping, running 4 or 5 wood rather than a long iron. But because the ball runs a long way, it's better not to aim for the flag if there's a bunker in your path. Often you can take a line to miss the trouble and still make it to the edge of a green.

FROM HEAVY ROUGH

When playing aggressively the clubface tends to close at impact. If you play the shot with a square blade you can easily hook the ball. To compensate for the club turning, lay the blade slightly open at address – this is one of the rare times the clubface isn't square to the ball-to-target line.

How much you open the club face depends on how tough and thick the grass is. Also take into account the amount of trouble there is around. Don't open the blade too much when the right hand side is packed with trouble – if the club doesn't turn the ball flies off right. When there's a lot on the left, make sure you open your blade enough to avoid going into it even if you do hit a slight hook.

Your downswing path is again steep which allows as little grass as possible between the clubface and the ball. But even if you hit the shot well, you can't apply any backspin on the ball from thick rough. Allow for a lot of run on the shot.

When playing from either light or heavy rough, strike firmly at the ball and never quit on the shot.

AVOID THE HOOK

Beware of the clubhead turning in your hands when playing from thick rough. If you lay the clubface square to the target the blade closes at impact and the result is a hook. To stop the hook, open the clubface at address. Opening the blade returns the face to a square position at impact. This is especially important when playing from wiry bermuda grass.

CLOSED CLUBFACE LEADS TO SNAP HOOK

SLIGHTLY OPEN BLADE FOR STRAIGHT SHOT

THICK ROUGH

SQUARE BLADE OFF FAIRWAY AND LIGHT ROUGH

OPEN BLADE IN THICK ROUGH RETURNS TO SQUARE AT IMPACT

BALL-TO-TARGET LINE

THICK ROUGH FORCES SQUARE BLADE TO CLOSE

Lyle's power play
The burly Scot Sandy Lyle has few problems with the rough. He manages to attack the flag even from heavy grass. With a steep attack his awesome power and excellent clubhead control mean he can cut through the rough without the fear of hitting a really bad shot. He used all his strength to cope with the grass at the 1989 Scottish Open, and finish as top placed Scot.

Exploring the fade

Many top players – including Nick Faldo, Lee Trevino and Jack Nicklaus – use the fade as their stock shot. Although you can't hit the ball quite as far with a fade as you can with a draw, you have greater control over the shot – as the ball has a high flight path and lands softly.

Hitting the fade for control and accuracy is not the only way to play this shape of shot. Make full use of the fade to set up birdie chances on awkward holes.

FADING FAVOURITES

You can play the fade to counter the effects of both slope and wind. If the fairway slopes from right to left and is hard and running, a straight shot or draw is likely to roll too far left and end up in the rough. But if you hit the fade the ball moves from left to right and runs slightly uphill on landing, which holds the ball on the slope.

Aim the clubface square to a tar-get on the left of the fairway and align left of the ball-to-target line so that when the shot cuts back it has plenty of room to work with. Even if the ball doesn't fade it shouldn't run too far into the left rough.

The fade is also useful to hold the ball in a right to left wind. Instead of aiming right of the target and letting the wind drift the ball back, set it off on a line just left of the flag and cut it back on to the target. The ball lands softly – especially helpful if the green is firm.

Play one or two clubs more than usual – depending on the strength of the wind – as the ball doesn't fly as far when cutting into it.

TARGET RIGHT

Hitting the left to right shot is also very useful for getting at a hidden target on the right.

Some dog-legs right are angled so sharply that you can hit only a long iron to the corner before running out of fairway. But if you hit a driver and move the ball from left to right you can slide a shot around the corner, leaving you with a much shorter second.

CONTROLLED SLICE

Exaggerate the fade – so it be-comes a controlled slice – to hit a shot around trouble, usually trees. The technique of the swing is almost the same as normal. The only difference is that your body aligns well left of the target but the clubface is still square to the ball-to-target line. The ball sets off well to the left of the target and cuts back a long way.

▼ **Playing the exaggerated fade is very useful when you haven't a clear shot to the target. By aligning left and aiming your clubface squarely at the flag the ball starts left of the trees and cuts back through the air towards the green.**

Hold the slope

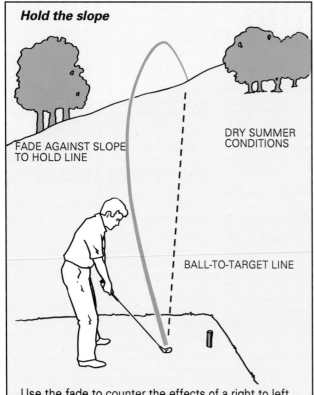

FADE AGAINST SLOPE TO HOLD LINE

DRY SUMMER CONDITIONS

BALL-TO-TARGET LINE

Use the fade to counter the effects of a right to left slope. A straight shot or draw is likely to run off to the left and into the rough. But a fade holds the ball on the slope. Align left with the clubface square to a target on the left of the fairway.

Counter crosswind

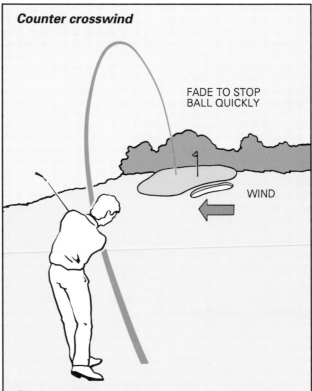

FADE TO STOP BALL QUICKLY

WIND

Playing one or two clubs more than usual, hit a fade into a right to left wind to gain control over the shot. Align slightly left and aim your clubface square. The ball cuts back into the wind, lands and stops quickly. A normal shot runs on landing.

Dog-leg driver

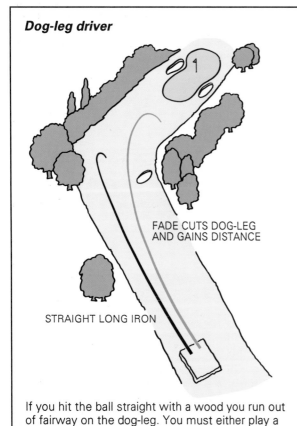

FADE CUTS DOG-LEG AND GAINS DISTANCE

STRAIGHT LONG IRON

If you hit the ball straight with a wood you run out of fairway on the dog-leg. You must either play a long iron to the corner or a long fade with a wood. Fading left with the wood leaves you with a much shorter second to the green.

masterclass

Faldo's fabulous fade

In the 1989 PGA Championship at Wentworth, Nick Faldo played a magical shot at the 15th hole to secure the title. After driving to the right he found he was blocked out from the green by trees. He had to aim about 60yd (55m) left of the green as he took his stance.

Using a 3 iron he hit a low cut shot some 200yd (183m) to within a few feet of the flag. A possible bogey became a birdie and he went on to win by 2 shots from Ian Woosnam.

Pitching

For a pitch shot, the ball is hit high and travels further in the air than along the ground. A pitch is an extension of both the medium and high chip shots and is played between 35yd (32m) and 100yd (91m) from the green.

The aim of a pitch is to play the ball close enough to the hole so that your next shot is a short putt. To play it well requires a lot of practice as well as a fine touch, but once you've mastered it you could save yourself several shots per round.

The pitch is a feel shot played with no more than a three-quarter swing and with any one of a number of clubs. The most common are the sand wedge, pitching wedge and 9 iron.

CHOOSING YOUR CLUB

The club you use depends on the distance of the shot. The sand wedge, with a clubface loft of about 56°, is for shots of 35-60yd (32-55m) while a pitching wedge (with a loft of about 50°) is for 61-80yd (56-73m) strikes. A 9 iron (about 46° loft) hits the ball 81-100yd (74-91m) with a three-quarter swing.

These distances increase as you improve. But whatever the distance of the shot and whichever club you use, your tempo must stay the same.

The technique is the same for

PITCHING TO YOUR TARGET
The pitch is a high shot played with a lofted club – the ball spends more time in the air than rolling along the ground. The key to a successful pitch is to keep your left hand, wrist and arm firm at impact.

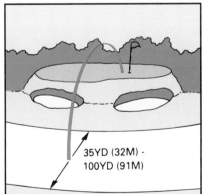

35YD (32M) -
100YD (91M)

The pitching zone
The pitch shot is played to a target between 35yd (32m) and 100yd (91m) away – and even further as your game improves. You have to hit the ball high from this distance because you are too far away to play the chip and run – even if there are no hazards between your ball and the target.

Vary your swing length

Providing you keep the same tempo for all shots, the length of your swing determines how far you hit the ball. To develop a feel for distance, vary your swing from half to two-thirds to three-quarters when practising – but keep the same tempo for each stroke.

each club – although the swing plane changes slightly according to the length of the shaft. The shorter the shaft the more your back is bent and the more upright the swing plane is. The sand wedge has a steeper swing plane than either the pitching wedge or the 9 iron.

ADDRESS AND SWING

Hold the club about 2in (5cm) down the shaft with the standard overlap grip. Take a slightly open stance with your left foot about 2in (5cm) behind your right, so that your hands and arms can swing freely through impact. However, your hips, chest and shoulders remain parallel to the ball-to-target line.

Your stance is slightly wider than if playing a chip and run. The ball is midway between your feet.

Let your left wrist break immediately you start the takeaway. This helps create a steep backswing and moves your hands and arms into the correct position to start the downswing.

Your left hand must stay ahead of the clubface on the downswing, and pull it into the ball. Keep both

hands, your wrists and arms firm as you hit the ball. At impact, both hands are still slightly ahead of the clubface – it is only after impact that it moves level with your hands. Your right hand stays behind the left for as long as possible.

It's vital to remember that your left hand dominates the swing,

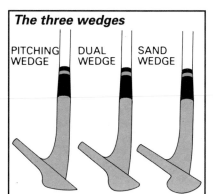

The three wedges

PITCHING WEDGE   DUAL WEDGE   SAND WEDGE

In addition to the sand wedge and pitching wedge, there is a dual wedge which combines the qualities of both. Its loft angle is midway between the two – and it has a rounded sole for bunker play. If you have all three clubs in your bag, practise pitching with each to feel the differences you achieve in height and length.

REDUCED BACKSPIN FROM ROUGH

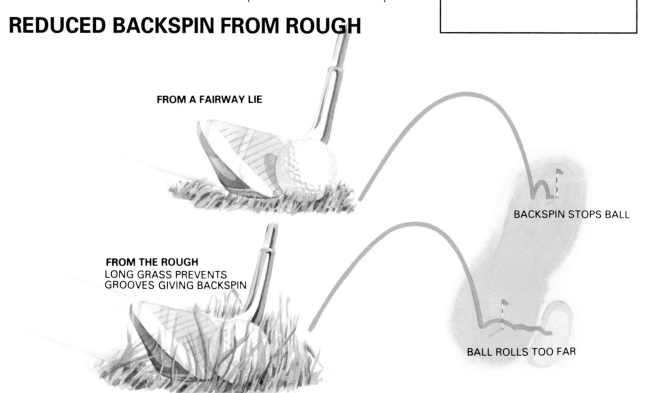

FROM A FAIRWAY LIE

FROM THE ROUGH
LONG GRASS PREVENTS GROOVES GIVING BACKSPIN

BACKSPIN STOPS BALL

BALL ROLLS TOO FAR

You can't generate much backspin when playing from the rough. This is because blades of grass become trapped between the clubface and the ball and stop the clubface

grooves from imparting spin. This results in a 'flier' and the ball doesn't stop quickly on landing.

Keep this in mind when pitching from thick grass. Try to land your

ball a few yards further back than normal and let it run up to the flag. Remember to visualize your shot carefully when playing from the rough.

PLAYING A PITCH SHOT

1 ADDRESS POSITION
Open your stance by sliding your left foot back about 2in (5cm) but keep your shoulders, chest and hips parallel to the ball-to-target line.

2 TOP OF BACKSWING
Make about a three-quarter backswing. The exact length depends on the distance of the shot. Your weight moves from an even distribution at address to your right foot.

3 THROUGH IMPACT
Keep your left wrist firm and focus on striking the back of the ball. Don't scoop it. Just after impact the clubhead moves level with your hands for the first time.

4 COMPLETION OF SWING
Your weight transfers on to your left side which lets your upper body rotate to the left to face the target. The throughswing is the same length as the backswing.

pro tip

Maintain hand speed at impact
When pitching from a difficult or rough lie be sure to hit through the ball at an even tempo. Don't shy away from difficult shots. Be aggressive at impact – if your hands slow down you fail to strike through the ball correctly. This leads to a poor hit and you will be lucky if your ball reaches even halfway.

while your right remains passive. This is the single most important point in pitching because your left arm and hand pull the clubface through the ball and so control its speed and path.

Let your body rotate to the left on the throughswing and allow your left shoulder to rise. From an even distribution at address your weight moves on to your right foot on the backswing, and on to the outside of your left foot by the completion of the swing.

A FIRM IMPACT

Your hands must be firm at impact to give you clubface control, direction and feel. Many golfers flick at the ball in an effort to gain height. Not only is this bad technique, it is also unnecessary. It's the loft of the clubface that gives your ball height.

As you practise, note that the s and wedge imparts more backspin than either the pitching wedge or the 9 iron. It has the most loft and creates a steep swing plane with its short shaft.

However, when learning to pitch, concentrate on selecting the club that hits your ball the necessary distance with a three-quarter swing. If the pin is close to a hazard don't risk forcing a sand wedge up to a full swing just because it imparts more backspin and stops the ball quickly. Take a longer club and accept that your ball will roll further on landing.

At this stage concentrate on developing a repeatable swing with all three clubs. Your backswing and followthrough must be of equal length.

OUT OF THE ROUGH

Pitching from long grass (rough) provides its own special problems,

PLAYING FROM THE ROUGH

1 OPEN CLUBFACE AT ADDRESS
Open the clubface slightly at address and grip the club firmly. This limits the amount it slips in your hands as the clubhead cuts through the rough.

2 FOCUS ON BACK OF BALL
Take the club away smoothly and break your wrists immediately to steepen the angle of the swing plane. Focus on cleanly striking the back of the ball.

3 LEFT HAND FIRM IN ROUGH
Your left hand takes the strain at impact as the rough gets entangled with the clubface, which turns to the left. This is why you open the clubface at address. Keep your head down through impact.

4 WEIGHT MOVES ON TO LEFT SIDE
Your weight transfers on to your left foot on the followthrough and your body rotates to face the target. Try to maintain your tempo throughout the stroke.

although the basic technique remains the same.

As the clubface passes through the rough, the tall, thick grass acts as a barrier and tries to twist the club in your hand to the left (clubface closes). Your left hand feels a greater strain at impact than if playing a pitch from the fairway.

You must counter the extra pressure exerted on the clubhead – and your left hand – by gripping the

club a little more firmly and opening the clubface slightly at address. Be sure to keep an even tempo throughout the swing.

Grass gets entangled between the ball and the clubface. This is unavoidable, so concentrate on hitting down on the ball and making as clean a strike as possible. Your swing path, stance, and ball position do not change when playing from the rough.

Punch Pitch

GREEN CONTROL
The punch pitch – one of the pros' favourites – is easy to control as your action produces a lot of backspin and the ball pulls up quickly on the green. Learning and being confident with this shot greatly increases your chances of getting up and down in 2 with your wedge – especially in a wind.

Controlling a wedge from the awkward distance of 50-90yd (45-80m) is a great asset. The punched pitch is the perfect shot to manoeuvre the ball through a wind from this range, but is by no means it's only use. All top golfers regularly hit this type of pitch both in windy and calm conditions to gain control.

The technique is simple and easily repeatable, which helps you play the stroke consistently well, provided you practise it. When hit properly the ball flies lower than a

PRECISE PUNCHING

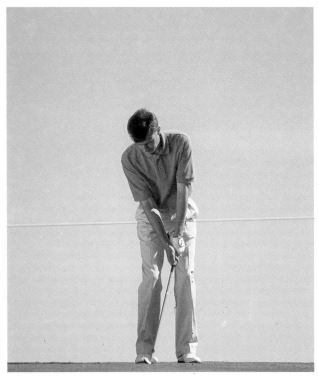

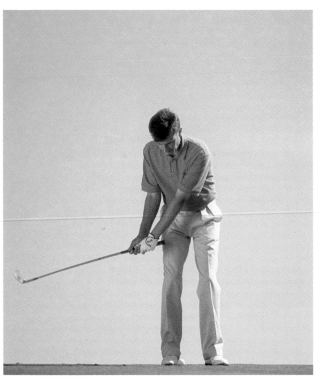

1 BACK ADDRESS
Grip down the club slightly for more control. Align parallel to the target line. Position the ball back in your stance – just inside the right foot for a very low punch. Aim the blade square to the target, and push your hands ahead of the ball. Distribute your weight evenly.

2 FIRM WRIST TAKEAWAY
Take the club away smoothly with little wrist break. Though the shot is mainly a hands and arms stroke you must still turn you hips and shoulders during the backswing.

normal wedge and stops quickly on the green, as the way you strike the shot naturally creates much back-spin.

FAVOURABLE FLIGHT

The boring, penetrative flight is invaluable when firing into a head or crosswind, but is equally useful with the wind at your back.

Instead of hitting a pitch and run or a high floating shot – both trusting a little to luck – you can afford to attack the flag by playing the punch pitch. Even though you're hitting downwind the ball should pull up quite sharply, but allow for some run depending on the firmness of the green.

The spin comes from a sharp downward blow on a ball that's placed slightly further back in the stance than normal. The action of striking the ball before the turf is important for the shot to succeed. A touch fat and the ball runs on landing – as little spin is produced – and control is lost.

The ball stays low because it is placed back in the stance with your

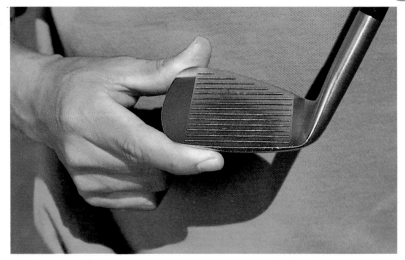

Wedge comfort
However good your technique is, you must also feel positive for the punched pitch to come off. For your confidence to be high it's vital to be comfortable with your wedge. There is no way that you can play the punch pitch well if your wedge doesn't suit you.

Knowing you have a club in your hand that you consistently strike out the middle of the face puts you in a positive frame of mind.

You may already have a favourite wedge -- often bought years ago – but if you don't, there are plenty of specialist wedges on the market. Finding a suitable one-off wedge means you needn't part with it when you change your set of irons.

3 SHORT AT THE TOP
Still keeping the wrists firm stop your backswing well short of parallel. Though the position at the top is not as long as usual, try to turn fully. Poor shoulder turn leads to an out-to-in downswing and a wayward shot.

4 SMOOTHLY DOWN
Swing down smoothly and keep your wrists firm. Too steep and wristy an attack makes the ball fly too high. Make sure your hands stay ahead of the clubface all the way to impact.

5 CRISP STRIKE
Lead the strike with your left hand and be sure to hit the ball before the turf. Keep your hands ahead of the clubface through impact and resist releasing, so the blade stays square for as long as possible.

6 SHORT AND BALANCED
Because you resist releasing your hands your extension is full and the followthrough short, which helps to keep the ball low and firing at the target. Don't stop too sharply as it leads to a stabbed shot. The finish should be balanced, with your weight fully on the left side.

hands forward, which delofts the clubface. The less wristy action than normal also helps to produce penetrative flight.

The punch pitch shot helps eliminate a miss-hit when playing under pressure, as the chances of hitting a thin or fat are less than with a straightforward pitch.

Reduced wrist action and having the ball placed further back in the stance both encourage crisp striking, so long as you don't dip too sharply on the downswing.

But for the shot to be accurate you must also be controlled on the followthrough. Lead with the left hand through the shot and avoid releasing too early. Try to keep the blade square to the target for as long as possible – this lessens the risk of a pull. Your finish position is much shorter than normal, but your whole action should be smooth.

WORK THE WIND

If you feel confident with this shot you can also shape the ball slightly to counter a crosswind. To produce a slight draw that holds on a left to right wind, stand a touch closed with the blade still square. But be sure not to use too much right hand as you could easily hit a hook.

If you open up your stance a fraction and keep the blade square the ball naturally fades slightly, which is useful in a right to left wind. The ball climbs a touch higher than the straight punch pitch and lands very softly – improving your control.

pro tip

Practice pitch
If you haven't tried to play the punch pitch before, it's sometimes hard to resist breaking your wrists on the backswing and through impact. One drill that is quick and easy to perform helps you naturally to keep the ball low and drilling.

Stick an umbrella into the practice ground, and pace out about 60yd (55m). From there, try to pitch balls – without bouncing – on to the umbrella and knock it over. This breeds an attacking and positive approach and helps you to hit the ball crisp and low – vital for punch pitch success.

José-Maria's wedge mastery
The brilliant Spaniard José-Maria Olazabal has worked his way to the top of world golf very quickly. His superb all-round game is capped by complete mastery of the wedge. He has tremendous natural flair and combines it with outstanding technique.

The punch pitch is an important weapon in Olazabal's armoury and makes him a deadly short game player. The dry, running fairways of Gleneagles in mid summer are the perfect surfaces for Chema to show off his prowess with the wedge. The short, controlled finish is a tell-tale sign of a low, spinning punched pitch shot that bites on the slick greens.

Chipping around the green

A chip is a stroke played from between 5yd (4 m) and 30yd (27m) of the green. The aim of a chip is to get your ball close enough to the hole so that your next shot is simply a tap-in with the putter. Good chipping can save you at least half-a-dozen strokes per round. With regular practice you'll find your chipping improves dramatically.

The chip is a short shot you play with two-thirds swing or less and it needs a deft touch to do it well. Although you can chip with any iron from a 5 down to a sand wedge – depending on the length of the shot and the obstacles to clear – this chapter concentrates on

PICKING THE SHOT

The type of chip you play depends on the situation you find yourself in. Assess the lie of the land for how far the ball can fly and how far you want it to roll. As a general rule

three of the most common types of chip using the 7 iron; 9 iron; and sand wedge.

WHICH CHIP?

Before choosing your chip, you must consider three factors: how high the ball needs to fly; how far it has to fly; and how far it can roll.

As a general rule you should always try to run the ball along the ground for as great a distance as the terrain permits, since there is less chance of the shot going wrong on the ground than in the air.

If the ground is relatively flat and even and there are no obsta-

always try to run the ball along the ground for as far as possible. This is easier and safer than trying to stop the ball quickly with a more lofted club.

cles to clear, then a low-flying chip and run is best. Play this shot using a clubface with little loft, such as a medium iron, so that the ball travels in a low trajectory (curving flight path through the air). The ball spends one-third of its journey in the air and the remaining two-thirds rolling along the ground.

If there is an obstacle to clear between you and the green but there is still quite a way for the ball to roll, play a medium height chip using a short iron. With this shot the ball spends roughly equal parts of its journey in the air and on the ground.

The ground between your ball and the green may be uneven with humps, bunkers or an irregular surface, and with not much level ground to the pin for the ball to roll over. In this case you want the ball to spend nearly all its time in

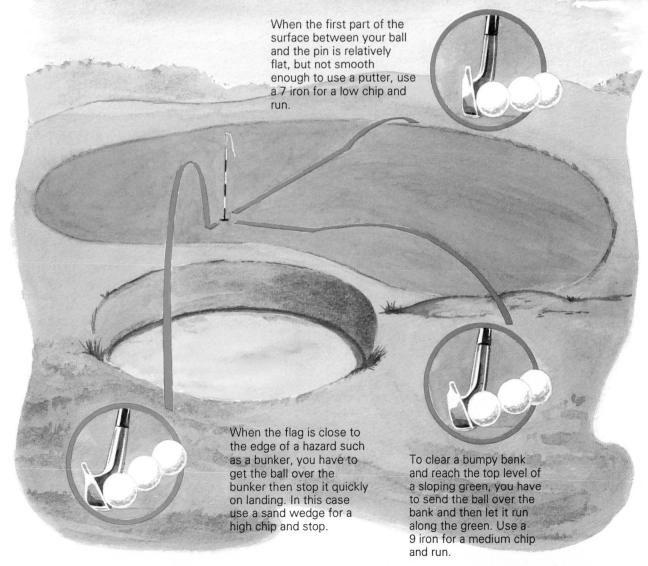

When the first part of the surface between your ball and the pin is relatively flat, but not smooth enough to use a putter, use a 7 iron for a low chip and run.

When the flag is close to the edge of a hazard such as a bunker, you have to get the ball over the bunker then stop it quickly on landing. In this case use a sand wedge for a high chip and stop.

To clear a bumpy bank and reach the top level of a sloping green, you have to send the ball over the bank and then let it run along the green. Use a 9 iron for a medium chip and run.

7 IRON CHIP AND RUN

1 AT ADDRESS
Use a putting grip down the handle. Move your left foot about 2in (5cm) back to open your stance but align your upper body parallel. Clubface aim is square to target. Your weight favours the left.

2 BACKSWING AND IMPACT
Do not break your wrists on the backswing. The clubhead reaches no higher than knee level at the top of the backswing. The swing is a pendulum movement similar to a crisp putting stroke.

3 THROUGHSWING
Your shoulders, arms and hands move as one during the whole stroke. Do not break your wrists on the throughswing which is as long as the backswing. Your left shoulder rises after impact.

the air before stopping quickly. Play a shot – commonly known as the chip and stop – where you send the ball high with a club that has a big loft angle, such as a sand wedge. With this shot the ball is in the air for at least two-thirds of its route.

CHIPPING BASICS

Regardless of the stroke you play and the club you use there are a few basics that apply to all chipping strokes. For a start, your back and throughswing are the same length. At the same time you need a longer back and throughs wing the further you have to chip. The slightest change in clubhead speed makes a great difference to the result of the shot. Practice will help you learn a feel for the ball and teach you how far you have to swing.

Another common feature of all chip shots is aligning your lower body left of the ball-to-target line. An open (aligned left) lower body prevents your hips from obstructing your hands at impact. For proper chip alignment take a normal parallel stance, and then slide your left foot back about 2in (5cm) to open your stance and align left.

However, you must still align your upper body parallel to the ball-to-target line. Also, the aim of the clubhead is always square on to the ball-to-target line.

THREE USEFUL CHIPS

Around the green there are three common situations you might find

yourself in. Each calls for a different chip. The first is where your ball is lying just off the green beyond the apron. Here you use a 7 iron and a low chip and run. Where your ball is slightly further away, with perhaps a bank in the way you can chip with a 9 iron. Finally, where

9 IRON MEDIUM CHIP

1 AT ADDRESS
Hold the club with a normal grip but still down the handle. Otherwise address the ball the same as for a 7 iron chip and run.

Chip tip
When you are playing a short chip and run, the stroke is crisp and firm and your wrists must not move forward of the clubhead. Lift your left shoulder on the throughswing.

your ball is lying with a bunker or some other hazard in the way and the hole is close to the hazard, use a sand wedge to play a high chip and stop to bring your ball close to the hole.

7 IRON LOW CHIP

Use this shot when there are no obstacles to clear and there is a large area of even ground for the ball to roll along. The ball travels two-thirds of its distance on the ground and only one-third of it in the air.

To play this shot, hold the club with a putting grip and grip down the handle. Aim the clubface square on to the ball-to-target line and adopt an open stance. Position the ball in the centre of your stance.

Do not break your wrists on the backswing, and let your shoulders, arms and hands move in unison during the whole movement. This produces a smooth action which should be short and crisp.

The swing is, in effect, like a crisper version of the putting stroke. By using the putting grip you eliminate wrist action. Try to imagine your swing as a pendulum motion with an equal length back and throughswing.

Your shoulders, arms and hands move as one unit from start to finish and the clubhead stays

IN THE AIR AND ON THE GROUND

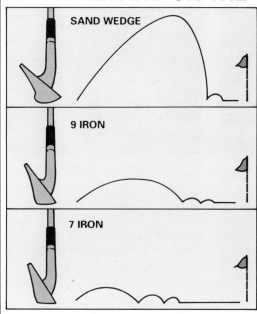

To help you select the right club for the chip remember that in a 7 iron chip the ball travels about two thirds of its journey rolling along the ground; with a 9 iron chip the ball is on the ground for half its journey; with a sand wedge chip and stop it is on the ground only for the last third of its journey.

square to the ball-to-target line during most of the stroke, only moving inside this line at the furthest point in both backswing and throughswing.

After impact allow your left shoulder to lift up. This stops your wrist from breaking and keeps the clubface square to the ball-to-target line for most of the followthrough.

The clubhead approaches the ball at a shallow angle, crisply sweeping it off the turf. This puts top spin on to maximize roll.

9 IRON MEDIUM CHIP

Use a 9 iron to produce a medium chip when the ball needs to be hit high enough to clear an obstacle, but doesn't need to stop quickly on landing. The curve of the ball is higher than that of a 7 iron – although it doesn't run as far along the ground.

With this chip use your normal grip but still grip down the handle. Set the clubface and address the ball in the same way as for the 7 iron chip.

2 BACKSWING
Break your wrists a little on the backswing and swing the clubhead to about waist height. Backswing is equal length to throughswing.

3 IMPACT AND ON
Allow your left shoulder to rise after impact so as not to let your clubhead overtake your hands. Hold your followthrough position.

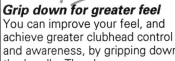

Grip down for greater feel
You can improve your feel, and achieve greater clubhead control and awareness, by gripping down the handle. The closer your hands are to the clubhead, the better touch you have, and the more accurate your shot.

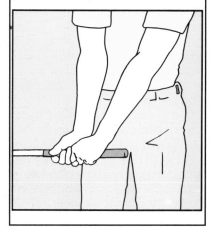

SAND WEDGE HIGH CHIP AND STOP

1 AT ADDRESS
Adopt the same grip and stance as you would for a 9 iron chip. Distribute your body weight evenly over both feet.

2 BACK AND DOWN
Allow your wrists to break at the start of the backswing which should be about two-thirds the length of your normal full swing.

3 IMPACT AND THROUGH
Your right hand must stay underneath the shaft to prevent any wrist roll. As you follow through, rotate to face the target.

This time let your wrists break a little during the backswing. At the top of the backswing your clubhead should reach no higher than hip level. The clubface attacks the ball at a steeper angle than the 7 iron and the clubhead follows a normal in-to-in swingpath.

Hold your followthrough and don't allow your wrists to break after impact. Let your left shoulder rise on the followthrough. As you complete the throughswing allow your upper body to rotate towards the target.

SAND WEDGE HIGH CHIP

Use the sand wedge to play the chip and stop. Select this club when the nearest landing point beyond a hazard is very close to the target – and when there is very little room for the ball to run. The sand wedge produces a high curve and creates backspin to stop the ball quickly. However, it is the least easy chip to perform because you have only a small area in which to land and stop the ball.

Grip the club and address the ball in the same way as you would for a 9 iron chip.

Let your left wrist break almost immediately as you start the swing. Your backswing is about two-thirds of the length of your normal swing. On the downswing the clubhead approaches impact at an acute angle, but don't let your hands overtake the clubface at any time.

Do not break your wrists through impact. Feel that your right hand is a passenger staying underneath the shaft as you strike. Your upper body turns to face the target at the completion of the followthrough.

CHIPPING PRACTICE

If you want to develop a good short game you must practise these strokes regularly. Not only do you need to learn the different techniques involved, but you have to acquire a feel for the shots. It is a general rule in golf that the shorter the shot, the more precise you must be and the greater feel you must have.

One good practice routine is to chip into an umbrella. Place the umbrella at the point where you want the ball to land. Position it at different distances and practise with different clubs – especially the sand wedge.

Another useful chipping practice aid is a chipping net. Use it in the same way as you would an umbrella, changing the distance away from you so you build up feel for the amount of swing needed.

When you become consistent at landing the ball in the umbrella or net, you are halfway to being a good chipper. The other half is achieved by correctly visualizing the shot – knowing where to land the ball and how it runs.

pro tip

Clubface control
To ensure that you do not flick at the ball through impact, your right hand stays under the shaft during impact and followthrough.

To pitch - or to chip

Pitches and chips are the shots that can make all the difference to your score by the end of the round. While both are played from anywhere between 40-100yd (35-90m), that is where the similarity ends.

A pitch is a high trajectory shot, usually played with a wedge, which lands the ball softly on the green. It's a useful shot for flying high over trouble. In wet conditions when the ground is soggy underfoot you can land the ball close to the flag and be confident of stopping it quickly.

A chip is the complete opposite and often played from closer range. A low flight means the ball is on the ground for about the same distance it's in the air. It's a good links shot – ideal when the wind is blowing or the greens aren't holding. A 7 or 8 iron is usually the best club for the job.

Choosing the right shot at the right time is one of the keys to successful scoring – it helps keep you out of trouble and can turn three shots into two. The factors which should make up your mind are the hazards and ground conditions between you and the green, and the strength and direction of the wind. Only when you've taken stock of the situation should you consider techniques.

HIGH FLYING PITCH

An approach shot over some form of hazard – whether bunkers, water or deep rough – is a situation you face on all types of course. Whatever the wind conditions, there's really only one way you can hope to finish close to the flag and that's to play a high pitch.

Think of the positive aspects of the shot to boost your confidence.

KNOWING WHAT'S BEST
There's more than one way to tackle almost every situation in golf. You can master the art of choosing the right one – just as the professionals do – providing you're aware of the conditions around you. When you're close to the green, the right approach can make all the difference between leaving you a holeable putt or a recovery chip.

The major benefit of pitching the ball on the green is that you can predict the bounce. This helps you attack the flag and removes any guesswork from the shot.

Remember, accuracy is all important – you must feel in control of the shot. Swing smoothly and strike with authority. There's seldom a call for hitting a wedge with all the force you can muster.

If there is trouble immediately beyond the green, play a high pitch to land the ball softly. The less run on the shot the slimmer the chance of the ball bouncing

CLEAR PATH: LOW CHIP AND RUN

1 ADDRESS PRECISION
There are no hazards in the 60yd (55m) between you and the flag. When the wind blows, the safest shot is usually the low chip and run – this is the stroke that gives you the greatest margin for error. Using a 7 or 8 iron, grip down the club and position your hands ahead of the ball. Bring your feet closer together than for a full shot, with the ball back in your stance. Use your imagination to picture the path of the ball all the way up to the hole.

2 HANDS AND ARMS SHOT
Swing your arms back and through with very little wrist movement. Pull the clubhead down and strike crisply into the bottom of the ball, pushing the back of your left hand low towards the target. Make sure your backswing is the same length as your followthrough to help you accelerate down into impact. The shallow angle of descent creates a tiny divot as the ball flies low, lands short of the green and runs up towards the flag.

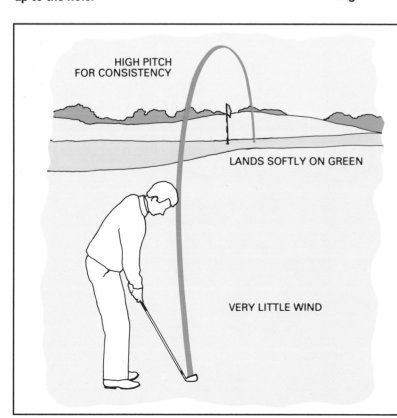

HIGH PITCH FOR CONSISTENCY

LANDS SOFTLY ON GREEN

VERY LITTLE WIND

Second choice
If the wind isn't blowing, a high pitch is an effective shot on any hole. You can accurately judge the flight of the ball and how it reacts on landing. Though the ground ahead is flat, there's no rule stating you must play a chip and run.

A great deal depends on how you visualize the shot. If you're under pressure – perhaps on a good score in a competition – it's crucial you play the shot you're most confident with. When a mistake might cost you dearly is no time for experimenting.

OVER TROUBLE: THE HIGH PITCH

1 WEDGE TO BETTER SCORES
The best shot to play in this situation is the high pitch – you can safely avoid flirting with the crater on the right. A chip and run may put you on the green, but it's a risky shot and difficult to judge when there's light rough ahead. Use your sand or pitching wedge depending on the distance you want to carry the ball. Stand square to the ball-to-target line and make a three-quarter backswing, breaking the wrists earlier than you would for a full shot.

2 FIRM STRIKE
Strike down firmly into the bottom of the ball, leading the clubhead with the back of your left hand to promote a steep angle of descent. Transfer your weight gradually on to the left side – driving your right knee towards the target helps you achieve this. Maintain a smooth tempo on the downswing – remember you should never force any shot, particularly an approach from close range. The clubhead strikes first the ball and then turf to create quite a large divot.

through the green into serious danger.

PERCENTAGE PLAY

When there are no hazards lying in wait you have the luxury of choice. In these situations it's important to play the percentages – choosing the shot that is least likely to go wrong.

In a strong crosswind your ball can easily be buffeted off line, particularly if you play a high pitch. With a stiff breeze behind or into your face distance can be difficult to judge accurately. The lower to the ground you keep the ball the less likely it is to be affected. A low chip and run is often the safest shot, but you need to be a little more creative than for a pitch shot.

Reach for a 7 or 8 iron and keep your swing simple. Visualize the ball landing on the fairway and running up towards the hole. Predict how humps, hollows or slopes

are likely to affect the path of your ball.

You may have to accept the occasional bad bounce which kicks your ball slightly off line. But it's unlikely to be one so severe that it makes the difference between hitting and missing the green.

TAKING CHARGE

If you learn to make the right decisions about when to pitch and when to chip, you're bound to

see an improvement in your scores. This course management ability has you thinking *before* you reach for a club. You find yourself hitting the ball close to the target more often and missing the green less.

But even the best golfers in the world – with experienced caddies alongside – make errors of judgement from time to time. Don't be hard on yourself if you make the same mistake twice, but include those specific points in your practice routine.

Shrewd swap for pitching
You can increase your short game repertoire by carrying a 60° wedge as well as your pitching and sand wedges. This extremely lofted club is ideal when you need to lob the ball high into the

air and stop it quickly.

If you already have 14 clubs in your bag you're likely to benefit from dropping one – perhaps your 2 iron – in favour of a third wedge.

HIGH ROLLER

1 ADDRESS POSITION
There's a hump in front of you and a two tiered green to negotiate, so you need to play a shot with a little height and plenty of run. An attempt to pitch the ball close to the flag is fraught with danger. From a fluffy lie, a sand wedge is the ideal club. Stand slightly open with your hands forward and the ball back in your stance.

2 SHORT BACKSWING
Pick the club up quickly on the backswing by breaking the wrists early. Tuck in your right elbow close to your side to increase your control over the club. Keep your backswing short – this encourages you to accelerate on the downswing. A little more than half your weight remains on the left side.

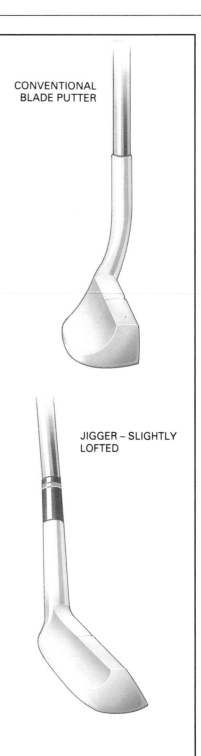

CONVENTIONAL BLADE PUTTER

JIGGER – SLIGHTLY LOFTED

3 STRIKE WITH AUTHORITY
Pull the clubhead down with your left hand to position your hands ahead of the clubhead at impact – this effectively reduces the loft of the club to ensure a lower flight. Focus your eyes on the back of the ball – you should strike firmly and with purpose. Stay down until the ball is well on its way.

4 THE RIGHT RESULT
Push the back of your left hand through towards the target to keep the clubface travelling in the right direction. Resist any temptation to let your right hand take charge of the swing. The ball pitches halfway to the flag and runs down the step in the green towards the hole.

Gentle loft for chipping
If you have problems with your chipping a jigger can give good results and restore your confidence at the same time.

Similar to the look of a blade putter, the jigger has a loft about the same as a 1 iron. Over closely mown grass you can use the club to play a low chip and run shot. The swing is simply an extension of your putting stroke – your grip and stance should be the same.

You may find you use this club more than one of the longer clubs in your bag, so weigh up the options and decide which is more beneficial to your golf.

Wedge off hard pan

During a dry summer the ground can become hard and bare – especially around the greens where golfers have trampled. Links courses are particularly prone to this problem.

The patches worn by the weather often cause problems for the inexperienced golfer when chipping. But as skills develop you should be able to play off hard pan without fear by using the correct techniques.

Whether you are faced with a bunker to go over or just a straightforward chip to the flag, your striking must be exact. Unless you nip the ball off the ground you can easily thin or fluff the shot.

LOB OFF BARE GROUND

If there's a bunker in the way, play the stroke with a pitching wedge to be safe. A sand wedge has a wide sole and may bounce into the ball. But you must still push your hands forward to lessen the risk of the pitching wedge doing the same. The club must strike the ball fractionally before the ground for a crisp strike.

Play the shot with very little wrist break – making timing easier – and from a central position to give the club as much loft as is safe.

If you hit slightly behind the ball the club may bounce into the back of it and you scull the shot. Quitting on the stroke usually means a duffed shot. Be confident

CRISP STRIKE
Playing from a hard, bare and awkward lie frightens many golfers – especially if you have to chip over a bunker. But by making a simple set-up change, and with sensible club selection, the shot can be played confidently and precisely.

Position the ball centrally in your stance to gain enough loft to take you safely over sand. Align slightly left and strike crisply. If your path to the flag is clear, place the ball back in your stance (below) and strike down firmly.

NORMAL CHIP FROM A BARE LIE

1 BACK FOOT ADDRESS
Position the ball opposite your right foot and square up the blade. Align slightly left of target and push your weight on to your left side. Grip lightly.

2 PUTTING BACKSWING
Play the stroke with a putting action. The backswing is short and controlled, and your wrists must remain firm. Keep your weight on the left side.

LOB OVER A BUNKER

1 CENTRAL POSITION
Place the ball centrally in your stance. This creates as much loft on the club as is safe. Square the blade and push your hands and weight forward. Align left.

2 WRIST BREAK FOR GREATER HEIGHT
Breaking your wrists a little on the backswing helps the ball gain height. But avoid too much wrist action as this makes timing difficult.

3 DOWNWARD BLOW
Strike down on the ball firmly, ensuring you hit it before the ground. Make sure you keep your hands ahead of the ball at impact, and don't break your wrists.

4 STIFF ARMED FOLLOWTHROUGH
Because you're chipping with a long putt action your followthrough should be short and your wrists still rigid. Your swing length varies with distance of shot.

3 LEAD WITH THE HANDS
Don't flick at the ball even though you need loft on the shot – you run the risk of thinning it. Keep your hands ahead of the ball and strike firmly.

4 FULLER FINISH
Make sure you don't quit on the shot. Follow through firmly and positively. The length of your throughswing should be the same as your backswing.

and strike firmly.

Never try to be too cute with the shot. Make sure you clear the bunker – a putt from 20ft (6m) behind the hole is far better than having to play from the sand.

CLEAR PATH

Even if the shot is free from obstacles, the dangers of thinning and fluffing remain. These problems can be ironed out by playing the shot with a pitching wedge from the back of your stance. Use a firm wristed putting action. Placing the ball back in the stance means you strike it with a firm downward blow – essential if you're to play the shot successfully.

Both shots need to be played with crisp confidence and poise – adopt a positive attitude rather than worrying over what could go wrong.

Safer shots
You can sometimes reduce the risk of fluffing or thinning the shot when playing from hard pan. With a lot of green to work with and a trouble free path to the flag, try running the ball along with a putter or a straighter faced iron. Use a putter only if there isn't much fringe to go over and the flag is quite a distance away. Play a 7 or 8 iron off the back foot if you need to clear a thick fringe.

Putter

7 iron

Beware the scull
Laying the blade too far open or catching the ground before the ball can lead to you hitting it thin. This sculled shot is destructive. The ball shoots past the flag, through the green and possibly into severe trouble.

Always play the wedge off hard pan by striking down on the ball and catching it first – then the ground. Trapping the ball between the ground and the clubface eliminates the danger of the thin or duff. Be firm – never try to be too delicate.

THINNED SHOT THROUGH THE GREEN

HARD BARE PATCH OF GROUND

masterclass

Watson's wonder wedge
Tom Watson is the master of links golf. His control and accuracy from the hardened, dusty ground are brilliant. Notice the controlled finish – his hands have stayed ahead of the clubhead throughout the stroke. The amount of dust thrown up shows how firmly he played the shot. He never quits on the stroke.

Watson's mastery helped him win five Open titles – he nearly equalled the Open record of winning a sixth in 1989.

Rough recovery play

On every course you can find different types of rough – dense and sparse, long and short, fairway and greenside. Alas, so can your ball.

If you're lucky, rough is no more difficult than playing from the fairway. But introduce a hazard or two, add a more challenging lie, and a recovery shot from rough is a demanding test.

Common sense is often more important than being a master magi-cian at shot making. Know what you can do and resist the tempta-tion to try any more. Don't risk turn-ing a minor mistake into a potential disaster – landing in even the most severe rough need never cause you to run up a high score.

Even Seve Ballesteros – a genius at recovery play – confesses he'd have more trophies on display in his living room if he'd known when to exercise a little self control earlier in his career.

OUT OF THE ROUGH STUFF
It's impossible to rehearse every recovery shot out of rough, because now and then you come across a totally unfamiliar lie. Your main thought must always be to find a safe route back to the closer mown grass – this is the first step away from disaster. By applying common sense to every situation, you can achieve a satisfactory result first time – and perhaps an even better outcome when you're next faced with a similar shot.

LIE MATTERS

Study the lie carefully – this has a tremendous bearing on how ambitious you can afford to be with your recovery. A vital point is that it's harder to control the ball from rough. Backspin is almost impossible to achieve and shaping the ball through the air is difficult.

Look at which direction the grass is growing around your ball. If the grass is with you (leaning towards the target) it's easier to strike the ball cleanly without making adjustments to your swing.

If the grass is against you a more precise strike is required. The clubhead must come down at a steep angle to prevent too much grass coming between the clubface and ball at impact.

Don't rule out the possibility of a flyer, particularly if the rough is wet. This can add yards to the flight of your shots.

A ROUGH RIDE

When you hit a tee shot into **rough lining the fairway**, survey the entire hole as you approach your ball. You then have a clearer picture of the situation when you come to prepare for the shot.

If the ball is sitting down, you may have to accept that the green is out of reach. Decide on a club you're confident with – one that guarantees a comfortable escape from the rough and puts you in a good position for your next shot.

If the green is in range, don't forget it's hard to apply spin from

Keeping watch
Make sure you keep an eye on your ball when it's heading for the rough. Don't turn away in disgust even though bad shots can be upsetting – your ball may prove very difficult to find in thick rough if you fail to watch it all the way.

Try to pick out a mark where the ball eventually comes to rest – perhaps a lighter patch of grass, a small tree or a different coloured bush. You can then walk straight to it and avoid holding up play.

FIRING THROUGH THE GAP

DECIDE ON THE SHOT
There's not much green to work with here, so concentrate on finding the putting surface rather than trying to place the ball close. When you size up the shot there are two points to consider – you must keep the ball low to avoid the overhanging branches but have enough height to carry the rough in front of you. Be careful – it's usually better to flight your ball too low than too high. If there's one stray branch jutting down lower than the others, a ball often has an uncanny knack of hitting it. You may then finish in an even worse spot.

1 SET UP TO HIT LOW
Choose a 9 iron for this shot and position the ball back in your stance opposite the right heel. With your hands pressed forward in front of the ball and the clubface aiming at the flag, you effectively decrease the loft of the club (above). This address position and the poor lie mean the ball comes out lower than normal.

rough, so pitch the ball short and allow for a little run on the shot. From a good lie you can almost afford to play your normal game, but you must still allow for less backspin. Don't expect to stop the ball quickly, even if it's lying cleanly.

SALVAGING SHOTS

In **greenside rough** the first concern is the lie. You should have a fair idea long before you reach the green – if you can see your ball from a distance you can expect a reasonable lie.

You immediately have a greater choice of shots open to you. Hazards shouldn't present you with a problem – you can safely negotiate your way around every form of obstacle.

If you can't see your ball as you approach it, prepare for the worst. A bad lie limits your options, so resign yourself to salvaging what you can without taking a big gamble.

2 SMOOTH PICK UP
Swing back smoothly along the ball-to-target line and allow your wrists to hinge (above). Don't take the club back outside the line – there's no need to cut across the ball with this shot. Stop the backswing when your hands are about waist high (below) – this is the perfect length to enable you to accelerate down into impact.

ON TO THE GREEN

3 STEEP ATTACK
You need to be extra firm from this lie or you risk moving the ball no distance at all. Strike down with your hands ahead of the clubhead (above). Even though you're using a lofted club, the slight variation in your technique ensures the ball flies fairly low. From behind, your impact position looks almost identical to address (below).

Check how much green you have to work with – if you're not sure of the exact distance, try standing to the side of your ball for a better view.

FLYING HIGH OR LOW

If there are bunkers to carry, a **high float shot** with a soft landing is called for, particularly if there's not much green to work with. Treat the shot much as you would if you were in the bunker – the same techniques in a different situation serve you well.

Adopt an open stance with the ball central, or slightly towards your back foot if the rough is very thick. Swing back steeply by breaking the wrists early and strike down firmly into the bottom of the ball. The clubhead cuts through the grass from out to in and the ball pops up high in the air.

You may have to play a **low trajectory shot** at any time – perhaps to avoid overhanging branches. Depending on the lie,

4 COMFORTABLE FINISH
Your left hand dominates before impact and it should continue to do so after the ball is on its way. Make sure the back of your left hand faces the target for as long as possible (above). This serves a double purpose – it prevents the clubface closing and guards against you scooping at the ball.

your club selection may vary from a long iron down to as little as an 8.

Judge the height and the amount of run you want on the ball and match the club best suited to the shot. Play the ball back in your stance and grip down the club for extra control. Strike down crisply, leading the clubhead into impact with your hands.

CALCULATED RISK

Much depends on the situation when you decide how ambitious you are with your recovery. If you're on a good score in a competition it usually pays to play cautiously. You can then limit the damage and move on to the next hole with your card intact.

In a relaxed game there's less at stake so you can afford to be more adventurous when you make your decision. You learn a valuable lesson whichever option you decide to take, and whether it's a success or not.

pro tip

On closer inspection
Identifying your ball in long or dense rough is sometimes a bit of a problem – thick grass easily conceals the manufacturer's name or number. If you're at all uncertain the rules allow you to lift the ball, check if it's yours and carefully replace it.

You must first announce your intention to someone in your playing group. This gives the player an opportunity to observe the correct lifting and replacement of the ball. If you fail to do so you incur a one stroke penalty.

CLEAN THROUGH
As you look up you're greeted with the sight of your ball flying low towards the target – safely avoiding the overhanging branches. You're likely to take no more than 3 shots from an awkward predicament.

Occasionally you take one less – it's then you start to notice how the ability to recover makes a difference to your score. It's also a tremendous boost to your confidence.

THRASHING AWAY TO SAFETY

1 ◄ OPEN UP
You can find some pretty wild rough on most courses. It's difficult to escape from but you can do better than hit and hope. Stand open with your shoulders, hips and feet aligning left of target. Aim the clubface at the flag. Grip firmly and further down than normal – hover the club above the ground to prevent the ball moving.

2 ► LEFT AT THE TOP
Make a full backswing along the line of your body to create an out-to-in swing path. Make sure your right elbow points down at the ground to help keep the backswing compact at the top. The club should point well left of target. Maintain a firm grip – particularly with the left hand – to prevent the club twisting when you swing down through the grass.

3 ◄ CUTTING EDGE
Generate plenty of clubhead speed coming down – you want to remove as much grass around the ball as possible. The out-to-in swing path combined with the cushion effect of the grass means the ball is unlikely to travel very far.

4 ▼ WRAP AROUND
Concentrate on completing your followthrough, even though you may feel some resistance from the wiry grass. Some of the dense rough is still tangled around the hosel of the club – this emphasizes the need to grip tightly throughout the swing.

The greenside bunker shot

The key to playing from a greenside bunker is to be positive – forget about the dangers of playing a bad shot. Don't be scared to attack the ball, even if the flag is only a few club lengths away. Most bad bunker shots are caused by being too hesitant – so the ball just trickles along the sand.

At first it's difficult to grasp a technique that moves the ball without a direct hit – the clubhead strikes sand. The shot takes courage, but you'll be surprised how easy and enjoyable it is when you've learnt the knack.

HITTING THROUGH SAND

Once you understand the mechanics and feel of hitting through sand, you're halfway there. The rest – as for every other shot in golf – is a question of addressing the ball properly and swinging the club correctly.

To get out of a bunker successfully, you have to gain enough height to clear the lip of the bunker and then stop the ball quickly on landing. For this, the sand wedge is ideal. Its rounded sole allows for an easy passage through the

LIFTED ON SAND

The greenside bunker shot is unlike any other in golf. At no time during the stroke does the clubface make contact with the ball itself. The clubface hits behind and underneath the ball, which is lifted by the momentum transferred through the sand from the clubhead to the ball.

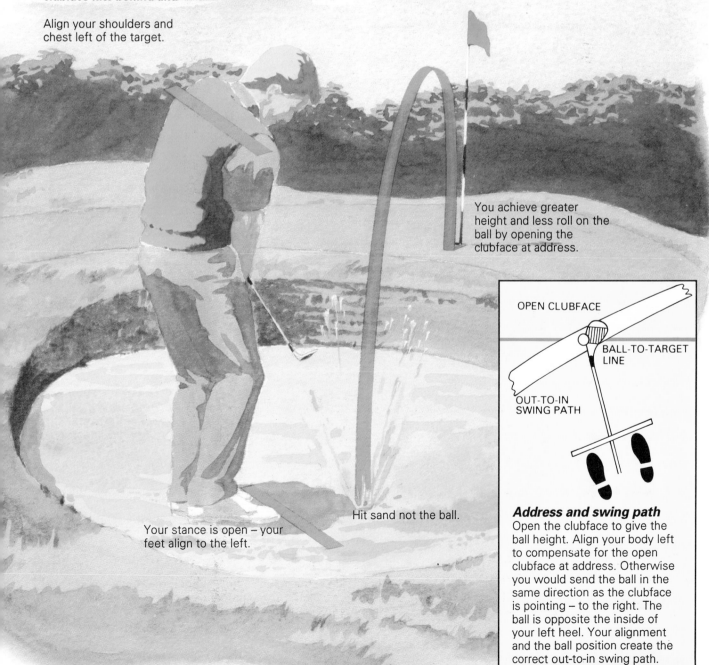

Align your shoulders and chest left of the target.

You achieve greater height and less roll on the ball by opening the clubface at address.

Your stance is open – your feet align to the left.

Hit sand not the ball.

OPEN CLUBFACE

BALL-TO-TARGET LINE

OUT-TO-IN SWING PATH

Address and swing path
Open the clubface to give the ball height. Align your body left to compensate for the open clubface at address. Otherwise you would send the ball in the same direction as the clubface is pointing – to the right. The ball is opposite the inside of your left heel. Your alignment and the ball position create the correct out-to-in swing path.

PLAYING OUT OF A BUNKER

1 SETTING UP
Open the clubface, grip down the shaft and take an open stance. At address, lines passing through your toes, knees, hips, chest and shoulders point left of target.

2 TAKE CLUB OUTSIDE BALL-TO-TARGET LINE
With the clubhead 1 in (4cm) behind the ball, take the club away outside the ball-to-target line – but don't touch sand. Break your wrists early on the backswing.

3 TWO-THIRDS SWING
At the top of the backswing your hands are no higher than shoulder height and your wrists are fully hinged. Rotate your body less than for a standard full swing.

4 OUT-TO-IN DOWNSWING
On the downswing let your arms and hands pull the clubhead from out to in. Keep your left wrist ahead of the clubhead to prevent the clubface from closing.

sand. Its loft angle – the greatest in the bag at 56-60° – puts height on the ball.

HOW THE SHOT WORKS

Instead of striking the ball, the clubface hits the sand behind the ball. It then passes through the sand under the ball. The momentum of the clubhead is transferred through the sand to the ball, which is lifted into the air.

The ball doesn't travel as far as if struck directly by the clubface. The sand between the clubface and ball acts as a cushion and by the time the power of the stroke reaches the ball it is greatly reduced. Despite the fact that the ball might travel a few club lengths only, this is still an attacking stroke.

ADDRESSING THE BALL

To play a greenside bunker shot, you set up with an open clubface and an open stance and body alignment. You then make a two-thirds swing with your club travelling in an out-to-in (right-to-left) swing path.

Hold the sand wedge in your right hand and open the clubface, so it aims right of target. The open clubface gives greater height to the ball, a softer landing and little roll.

When you've set your aim open, add the correct left-hand grip – slightly lower than usual to improve feel of the clubhead – and remove your right hand. Then add the correct right-hand grip. Always open the clubface before adding the correct grip.

You mustn't ground the clubface at address, so hold it just above the sand. The clubface should be about 1 in (4cm) behind the ball. Stand so that your feet are shoulder-width apart, with the ball opposite the inside of your left heel.

SWING AND SWING PATH

Adopt an open stance by standing with your left foot dropped back from the normal parallel alignment position. The rest of your body is also aligned left so that lines passing through your toes, knees, hips, chest and shoulder all point left of the ball-to-target line. Stand so that just over half of your weight (60%) is on your left foot. This set-up automatically produces the correct out-to-in swing path.

Smoothly take the club away outside the ball-to-target line. For the controlled two-thirds swing, swing the clubhead back until

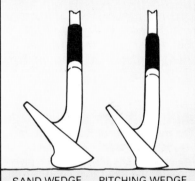

Which wedge?
The sand wedge, with its rounded sole, slides through sand, making it the best club for bunker play. If you don't have one, use the next most lofted club – the pitching wedge. The sharper-edged pitching wedge meets with more resistance from the sand, which reduces clubhead speed, but its loft should give you the height to lift the ball over the lip of the bunker.

SAND WEDGE   PITCHING WEDGE

5 STRIKE UNDERNEATH AND BEHIND BALL
Strike 1 in (4cm) behind the ball so that it explodes out on a wedge of sand. Your weight favours your left foot throughout the stroke.

6 MAKE FULL FOLLOWTHROUGH
After impact the club continues to move inside the ball-to-target line. Make a full followthrough to prevent stopping on the stroke.

your hands reach shoulder height at the top of the backswing. The precise length of the swing varies with the distance of the pin from the bunker. Practice will help you develop the feel for how long your swing should be.

Bring the club down on an out-to-in line so that the clubface travels from right to left through impact, entering the sand about 1 in (4cm) behind the ball. The clubface travels under the ball and re-emerges in front of the point where the ball was at address.

It is vital to keep the clubface moving through the sand at the same tempo as the rest of the swing. Exaggerate the through-swing to begin with to make certain that you don't stop on the shot – sand resistance slows down club-head speed. Keep your weight on your left side throughout. Practise hitting through the sand until you become confident.

SPLASHOUT ON THE SAND

The most important rule in bunker play is to hit sand not the ball. It is the force of the clubface as it passes through the sand that creates the power to splash the ball out – amid a shower of sand. The clubhead travels faster than the ball. Note how the clubhead is ahead of the ball.

HIT UNDERNEATH THE BALL AND AT LEAST 1½IN (4 CM) BEHIND IT

pro tip

Undercut your scorecard

One way to learn the technique is to place a ball in the centre of a scorecard in a bunker. Then swing the clubface under the card. This ensures you hit sand not the ball.

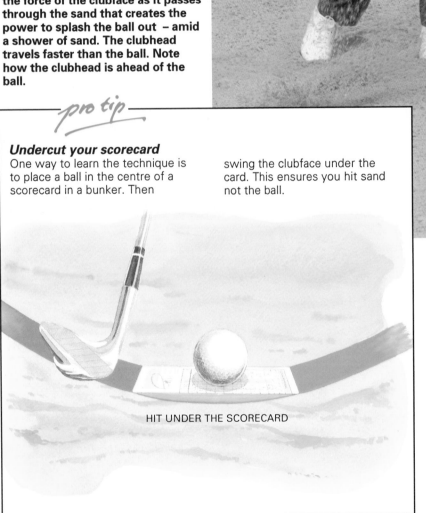

HIT UNDER THE SCORECARD

Testing the sand depth

Always test the depth and texture of the sand before playing a shot. Do this by wriggling your feet as you take your stance. If there's only a shallow layer of sand – a crust of solid mud, clay or hardened sand might exist just below the surface – your spikes don't move freely.

This test tells you how far under the ball your clubhead can pass.

Sloping bunker lies

Level greenside bunker lies present a tricky problem – upslopes and downslopes in the sand are often worse. You have to take exactly the correct amount of sand if you're to clear the face of the bunker and pitch the ball in the best place on the green.

UPSLOPES

When your ball is resting on the upslope of a bunker, the main point to remember is that the shot travels higher but covers less distance than from a level lie.

To fight this, change your technique by striking with a fuller swing than usual. Confidence is vital – many players are too cautious from an upslope, so the ball finishes a long way short of the hole.

DOWNSLOPES

If your ball rests on a downslope, the chances are that it has just trickled in. This makes your shot harder because the edge of the bunker – just behind the ball – impedes your backswing and

downswing.

The ball is sure to have a reduced angle of flight path, and rolls on landing. This is because downhill lies deloft the clubface. It's vital to remember this – and adjust your technique accordingly – when you play this shot.

JUDGE IT CAREFULLY
When your ball is lying on a slope near the front or back edge of the bunker it's an awkward shot to play. Tackle an upslope by opening your stance and body alignment but aim square to the target.

UPHILL SLOPE IN A BUNKER

1 SLIGHTLY OPEN STANCE

Set up with the clubface square to the target and an open stance. The ball should be on the inside of your left heel – this helps create extra loft so that you are confident of clearing the bank. Keep your hands just ahead of the clubhead. Good tempo is vital. A longer, even swing applies power – a hurried stab at the ball does not.

2 WEIGHT ON RIGHT
Take the club away smoothly. Stand at 90° to the slope – this helps you feel as if you're playing from a flat lie. Don't lean into the slope or you dig the clubhead deep into the sand on the followthrough.

3 KEEP YOUR TEMPO
The ball flies higher but covers less distance than a level bunker shot, so compensate by making a fuller backswing than normal. As the downswing begins, keep a steady tempo. Let your left wrist and arm lead the club.

4 CONSTANT CLUBHEAD SPEED
Maintain momentum through the ball – your aim is to let a wedge of sand lift the ball up and out. Don't let the clubhead slow down. Make contact with the sand about 1½in (3cm) behind the ball.

5 OBSTRUCTED FOLLOWTHROUGH
The upslope helps your ball gain height so the shot should not be ruined if the upslope or the bank prevents a full followthrough. Your weight still just favours your right side.

DOWNHILL SLOPE

1 OPEN CLUBFACE
Open the clubface as much as possible – this helps the ball to gain maximum height so that it clears the face of the bunker and stops more quickly. Align left to compensate for the clubface position and lift the club up sharply.

2 STEEP BACKSWING
Your immediate wrist break produces a steep swing path and guarantees that you don't incur a penalty by touching the hazard. It also helps you make a steep attack down on the ball so that it's forced up. The ball must be well back in your stance.

Don't hit the hazard

If you ground the club in the hazard, or hit the sand on your backswing or downswing, you incur a 2 stroke penalty. Play out of the bunker sideways – or backwards – if you're in any doubt at all about the club's path. Striking the grassy bank – above the border with the sand – does not incur a penalty.

Be extra careful not to touch the surface with your club if you fail to free your ball from the sand at the first attempt. Your ball is still in the hazard, so the rule still applies – even after impact.

The best of players sometimes forget this. Top pro Howard Clark once had a nasty bunker lie and failed to escape in one. In disgust, he stabbed his club into the sand – and had 2 strokes added to his steadily increasing score.

CLUB HITS GRASSY BANK – NO PENALTY

3 STRIKE BEHIND THE BALL
Your weight automatically favours your left side, so that you stand at 90° to the slope. This helps you feel as if you're on a flat lie. Strike about 1 in (3cm) behind the ball, ensuring that you take some – though not much – sand.

4 FULL FOLLOWTHROUGH
Make a full followthrough – you need to do everything possible to lift the ball up and over the face of the bunker. Because of the downslope the ball is sure to run on landing – take this factor into account when you prepare for the shot.

LOOK AT YOUR SHOT FIRST
From a bunker's downslope, the ball is certain to roll on
landing. Spend a few seconds – no more or you delay
play – visualizing the shot in your mind. Pitching the
ball to a precise spot is tricky – you need as much green
as possible to roll the ball on, but you must also strike
with enough power to clear the bunker. Keep a firm
mental image of the shot in your mind as you play.

Grip down for clubhead feel

Make sure that your hands take up their position
lower down the grip than usual. This promotes
your feel for the clubhead as you swing through
the ball – vital if you're to take the proper amount
of sand.

Hitting thin means that the ball either stays in
the bunker or skims through the green. If you
strike fat you may not even move the ball. Good
clubhead feel reduces the likelihood of these
disasters.

pro tip

Firm footing
As you take your stance to
play the shot, make sure
that your feet are firmly
embedded in the sand.
This helps you to keep
your balance through the
stroke, which is made
harder than usual by the
slopes. You must be
comfortable, standing at
90° to the slope to give
the feel of playing from a
flat lie.

Planting your feet
solidly also serves as a
gauge for sand texture –
use it to judge how the
clubface will pass through
the sand.

The fairway bunker shot

A fairway bunker shot is the most varied in the game. A fairway bunker is separated from the green by fairway or rough, and can be anything between 20yd (18m) from the target to 300yd (274m) or more away.

The wide range of distances is reflected in the clubs you can use – any one from a fairway wood to a sand wedge. However, the technique stays the same.

The club you choose depends on the position of the ball in the bunker and the distance between the ball and the target.

CLEAN STRIKE FOR LENGTH
To hit the ball a long way from a fairway bunker – a difficult shot – you must nip it off the top of the sand as cleanly as possible. It's a precision stroke with a lot at stake – success lands you on the green but failure leaves you still in the bunker and even worse off.

CHOOSING YOUR CLUB

Before choosing a club, assess how high the ball must fly to clear the front lip of the bunker. Visualize a straight line between the ball and the highest point on the lip. The nearer the ball is to the front of the bunker, the higher the lift it needs, and the greater loft the club must have.

Shifting your weight

Practise hitting fairway bunker shots with most of your weight on your right side by keeping your right foot firmly planted on the ground on the backswing and downswing. Don't let your right heel lift until after impact.

This routine delays the natural forward leg movement on the downswing, stops your weight shifting from right to left too soon and prevents the clubface striking sand.

5 IRON

If you're, say, a 7-iron distance from the green but need an 8 iron to clear the lip, don't gamble with the lower numbered club. You won't get enough elevation and the ball will strike the front face of the bunker – ending up in a worse position than before.

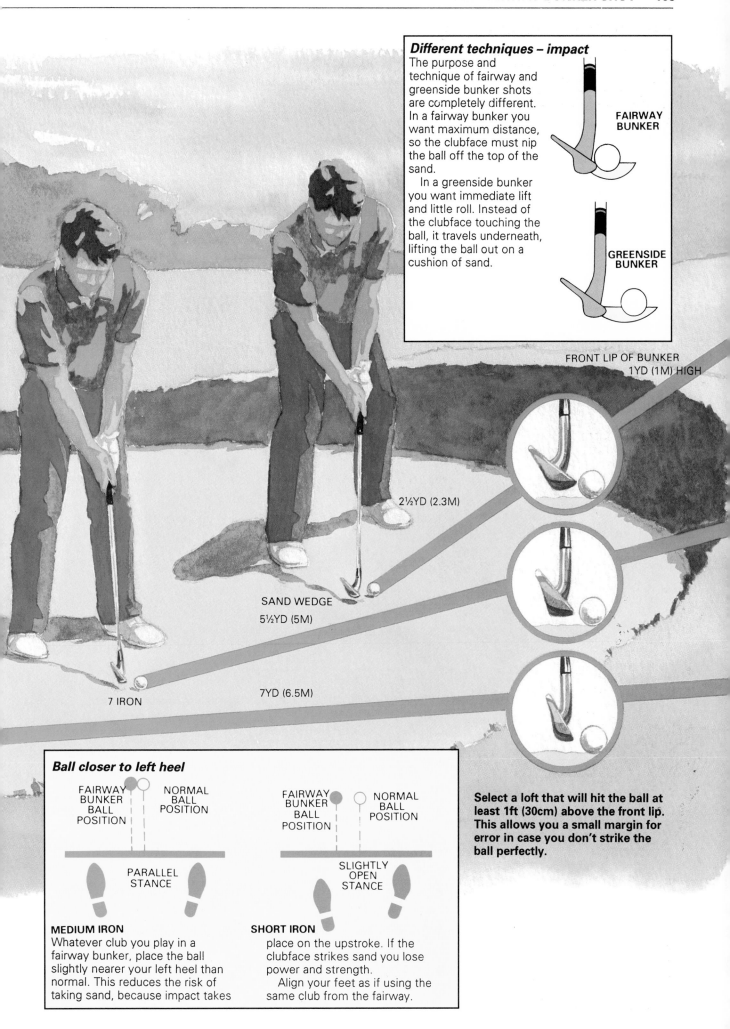

Different techniques – impact

The purpose and technique of fairway and greenside bunker shots are completely different. In a fairway bunker you want maximum distance, so the clubface must nip the ball off the top of the sand.

In a greenside bunker you want immediate lift and little roll. Instead of the clubface touching the ball, it travels underneath, lifting the ball out on a cushion of sand.

FAIRWAY BUNKER

GREENSIDE BUNKER

FRONT LIP OF BUNKER
1YD (1M) HIGH

2½YD (2.3M)

SAND WEDGE
5½YD (5M)

7 IRON

7YD (6.5M)

Select a loft that will hit the ball at least 1ft (30cm) above the front lip. This allows you a small margin for error in case you don't strike the ball perfectly.

Ball closer to left heel

FAIRWAY BUNKER BALL POSITION   NORMAL BALL POSITION

PARALLEL STANCE

FAIRWAY BUNKER BALL POSITION   NORMAL BALL POSITION

SLIGHTLY OPEN STANCE

MEDIUM IRON
Whatever club you play in a fairway bunker, place the ball slightly nearer your left heel than normal. This reduces the risk of taking sand, because impact takes

SHORT IRON
place on the upstroke. If the clubface strikes sand you lose power and strength.

Align your feet as if using the same club from the fairway.

HITTING FROM A FAIRWAY BUNKER

1 ADDRESS
Grip down the club and aim square. Adopt a normal stance for the club with the ball nearer your left heel than usual and with just over half your weight on your right side. Keep the clubhead above and behind the ball.

2 TAKEAWAY
Be careful the clubhead doesn't brush the sand on the takeaway. To create a wide swing plane, avoid breaking your wrists too early. Your hands, arms, shoulders and chest move together.

WHICH CLUB TO PLAY?

When assessing a fairway bunker shot, you must work out the height needed to clear the front lip of the bunker and the distance that your ball has to travel to reach the target.

First you need to consider clearing the bunker lip. The closer the ball is to the front of the bunker the greater height it needs to clear the lip. Work out which clubs have enough loft to hit the ball above the lip. Then choose your club.

If you can reach the target from your position, select the club with the most loft that also gives the perfect distance. Using the *highest* numbered club gives you the best chance of clearing the front lip of the bunker.

If you can't reach the target, maximum distance is usually your priority. Choose the *lowest* numbered club that gives your ball enough height to clear the front lip of the bunker.

Club selection is as important as making the correct swing. Assess the facts coolly before making a fairway bunker shot. Don't be greedy – a gamble rarely succeeds. Your ball usually stays in the bunker but in a worse position than before.

3 THREE-QUARTER BACKSWING
Make a controlled three-quarter backswing, turning your upper body 90°. At the top of the backswing your wrists are fully hinged. Don't be tempted to make a full swing or you may lose rhythm.

6 WEIGHT SHIFT
Only after impact does your weight transfer to your left side. Your upper body and head rotate to face the target. Maintain your normal tempo throughout the swing.

5 IMPACT ON UPSTROKE
Impact is on the upstroke. This gives you a cleaner strike than normal, as well as full benefit from the clubface loft for height to clear the bunker lip.

4 WEIGHT STAYS ON RIGHT SIDE
As your hands, wrists, arms and the clubhead approach the ball, more than half your weight is still on your right side. This stops the clubface from hitting too far behind the ball and taking sand.

A CLEAN STRIKE

The fairway bunker technique is the same for every club. The aim of the stroke is to pick the ball cleanly off the top of the ground – without the clubface touching the sand.

If sand gets trapped between the clubface and the ball it acts as a cushion, slowing the clubface down at impact, and loses you power and distance. There is also a 2-shot penalty if any part of the club touches the sand before impact.

For a clean strike, have the ball slightly nearer your left heel than normal. This means that impact is on the upstroke, so the clubface is moving up and away from the sand when it meets the ball. You also gain maximum benefit from clubface loft.

If you position the ball normally the clubface moves into the ball on the downstroke, increasing the risk of striking sand.

ADDRESS AND WEIGHT SHIFT

Having chosen the club, grip about 1in (2.5cm) further down the shaft than normal for greater clubhead control. Aim the clubface square to the ball-to-target line.

Align your body normally for the club but with the ball slightly nearer your left heel. Address the ball with just over half your weight on your right side, to help you strike the ball on the upstroke. This prevents your weight shifting on to your left side too early on the downswing and stops the clubface striking the ball on the down-stroke.

Although your upper body turns fully during the swing, leg action is restricted because of your weight distribution at address.

If your weight is distributed evenly at address, the natural forward movement of the swing and your body brings the clubhead into the ball too steeply and too early – and you take sand.

How ever far from the green you are, always make a three-quarter swing. This helps you maintain a good tempo, and makes it easier to achieve a clean contact.

PLAYING SAFE

Never force a full shot. For insta-nce, a 7 iron may have the least loft available to clear the front lip but would still leave your ball short of the green. Don't lengthen or increase the speed of your swing in an attempt to make up those extra yards. Accept that you'll be short and aim to save par with a chip and putt.

Playing safe is particularly impor-tant when your ball is very close to the lip – possibly so close that even the loft on a sand wedge won't give you quick enough lift to clear it. In this case, you must give up all

thought of sending the ball far and instead use the greenside bunker technique to play out.

Using the same club – a sand wedge – the greenside bunker shot provides almost vertical ele-vation, floating your ball out on a wedge of sand.

Playing from wet sand
Surprisingly, you get a cleaner strike from wet sand than from dry sand. This is because wet sand is firmer and the ball perches on top of the surface – just as it does on the fairway. The ball is easier to hit because you see more of it, and there's less risk of taking sand at impact – and of touching sand at address or takeaway.

INCREASE CLUBHEAD AWARENESS

GRIP DOWN
For better clubface control, grip about 1in (2.5cm) further down the shaft than normal. The closer your hands are to the ball, the greater your feel for the clubface is.

PENALTY POINT
Don't let any part of the club touch the sand before you hit the ball – or you face a 2-stroke penalty. This rule applies to all sand bunker shots.

A wood from the bunker

It's frustrating when your ball lands in a fairway bunker, particularly if you've notched up a good score. But be positive – all is not lost.

A well negotiated strike could land you in a position to save shots. Most fairway bunkers are shallower than those beside the green – and are often less difficult than they first appear.

Be flexible over your choice of club – an inspired shot is often the result of creative club selection. If the ball is sitting up well a fair distance away from the front of the bunker, it is much easier to get out using a utility wood rather than the more usual iron.

The small head and low centre of gravity of the wood allow more weight to pass underneath the ball and so lift it up quickly. And the smooth rounded shape of the head prevents snagging in the sand which often happens with the long irons.

CLUB CHOICE

One of the keys to success with a fairway bunker shot is choosing the right club. An iron is the obvious choice – but in many situations the wood may give a better combination of lift and distance.

Weigh up the facts carefully – enter the bunker, take your stance to the ball and visualize the shot coming out. You must decide which club is best for getting over the lip of the bunker *and* reaching the green. To work out the lift, consider how far the ball is from the front of the hazard.

The 5 wood lifts the ball higher and sends it further than a 2 iron, because it has more loft and a longer shaft. But if you feel that a wood is not going to clear the bunker, play safe – take a lofted iron instead.

ASSESS THE LIE

It's important to study the lie of the ball carefully. If the ball is sitting down or partly buried in the bunker, choose a lofted iron club and play a safe shot. But if the lie

FAIRWAY BUNKER WOOD
Use a utility wood to good effect to lift the ball up and over the lip from a fairway bunker lie. Grip down the club to compensate for the lower position of your body. A shorter swing and lower grip reduce distance but give greater control. To avoid a 2-stroke penalty remember not to ground the club at address or on the backswing.

MAKE A CLEAN STRIKE

1 **SET-UP**
Take a normal stance – wriggle your feet for a firm footing in sand. To hit cleanly focus your eyes on top of the ball before taking the club away slowly and surely.

2 **CONTROLLED CONTACT**
Make a three-quarter back and throughswing to increase your control. Keep a smooth rhythm to help you swing firmly down and through the ball.

3 **BALANCED FINISH**
After you've swept the ball cleanly from the sand, aim for a balanced finish. Keep your head still until your right shoulder forces it to turn and watch the ball's flight.

is reasonable and you have a good distance between the ball and the front of the bunker, pick a 5 wood – or even a 7 if you normally carry one.

POSITIVE APPROACH

After you select your club and take your set-up, be single minded in your approach – block out distractions and focus purely on your objective. Set aside thoughts of failure – a positive approach gives a better chance of achieving your target.

Take a firm footing in the sand – to avoid a 2-stroke penalty, remember not to ground the club at address. Grip down the club for extra control and sweep the ball cleanly off the sand with a smooth and purposeful three-quarter swing.

masterclass

Bunker courage
One of the most memorable shots of all time was played at the 1983 Ryder Cup. By the 18th hole the singles match between Seve Ballesteros and Fuzzy Zoeller looked as if it could go either way.

On this final hole, Seve played his drive to the left of the fairway to avoid water – only to find the fairway bunker. He needed to carry the ball some 250yd (230m) over water to reach the green. The risk was high.

Coolly assessing the situation, Seve chose a 3 wood and sent the ball searing over the face of the bunker. As it landed on the green the crowd roared in appreciation. Jack Nicklaus said it was one of the finest shots he'd ever seen.

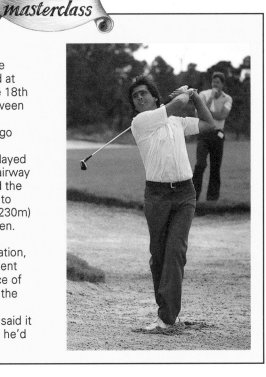

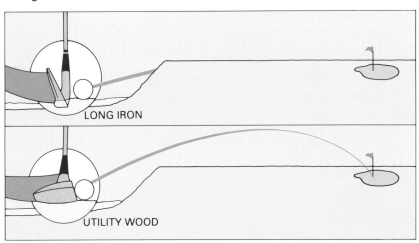

LONG IRON

UTILITY WOOD

Off the sand
With its rounded head and low centre of gravity, a lofted utility wood lifts the ball quickly and provides the necessary distance for a fairway bunker shot to reach the green.

The long irons have narrow soles which may dig into the sand – the ball is likely to end up at the side of the bunker.

Plugged lies

When your ball is sitting up in a bunker, you have a relatively simple shot. Plugged lies are another matter – extracting a buried ball from the sand is a tricky prospect.

Your ball could plug for a number of reasons. The texture of the sand is critical – newly laid sand can give you problems because it hasn't had a chance to settle.

Thick sand is likely to absorb your ball before the sand has time to thin out. When it does become finer, it acts as a cushion.

STUN SHOT

It's always the power of the club through the sand that blasts your ball out of the bunker – never try to play the ball itself.

With a ball that's lying well, you open the face, align left and use a fairly long swing. This provides height and backspin, so that the ball stops quickly.

The opposite happens when your ball is plugged. You set up parallel to the ball-to-target line with a slightly closed clubface.

That's why you can't expect height – the closed clubface digs

LESS HEIGHT THAN USUAL
Hitting successfully from a plugged lie is awkward because you don't get as much height and backspin as with a standard splash shot. Play a stun shot with a closed clubface to check the roll.

ESCAPING FROM A PLUGGED LIE

2 HALF BACKSWING
Swing back about halfway, breaking your wrists straight away. You need a steep angle of attack into the sand – the wrist break ensures it. When you play from a good bunker lie, your backswing is longer.

1 CLOSE THE CLUBFACE
Stand parallel to the ball-to-target line with the ball central. Close the clubface – this helps dig out the ball. Set up differently from your normal splash shot address – for a good lie – when you align left with the ball forwards and open the clubface.

GOOD LIE

Don't hit yourself
You incur a 2-stroke penalty if the ball touches you at any time – so be on the lookout for rebounds.

If the ball is plugged in the lip of the bunker, consider playing out sideways. It's better to escape anywhere than to attempt too hard a shot – you might be looking down at yet another bunker lie, which leaves you in an even worse situation.

out the ball effectively, but with very little lift. The ball emerges with top-spin and runs on landing to reduce further your chances of landing close to the flag.

To compensate for the strong roll, you must play a stun shot. This means having the confidence to cut short your throughswing, so that the clubhead does not pass your hands at any time.

Carefully assess the situation before you take up your stance, because the ball doesn't rise as well as from a good sand lie. You may not escape if the bunker has a steep face. If the face does look forbidding, play out sideways – at least you'll be out of the trap in one.

Strike firmly if you want plenty of roll. Trying for hardly any run on the ball is a riskier shot because you need to hit more softly – but

4 KEEP LEFT WRIST FIRM
Strike about 3in (7cm) behind the ball. At impact your hands should still be ahead of the clubhead with the left wrist – which mustn't collapse – taking the force of the shot. With a normal shot (right), the clubhead catches up with your hands at impact, but the role of the left hand is again vital.

3 HANDS LEAD THE CLUBFACE
Let your hands lead the clubface – exactly as you do when you're splashing out normally – and keep your left wrist dominant throughout the downswing.

not so softly that the club slows down, leaving your ball in the sand.

Although you strike with less power for the short hit, keep your left wrist firm. This helps to prevent slowing down the club as it enters the sand. When tempo is erratic, so is timing – and your shot is certain to suffer.

FIRM HOLD

Grip pressure is important. It should be firm for a long shot and more relaxed – though still solid – for a shorter shot.

It's worthwhile to spend some time in the bunker rehearsing strokes from a plugged lie. The more confident you are the more daring you can afford to be – but your top priority is to escape in one shot.

5 LOW CLUB AFTER IMPACT
Shorten the throughswing. This stunning action reduces the roll of the ball when it lands. From a good lie you don't need to lessen the followthrough, as the ball's height stops roll.

HOW'S IT LYING?

ASSESS THE SITUATION
When you enter the bunker, visualize your shot carefully. You can move man-made obstructions, but natural impediments must be left as they are. It's possible that you can move stones without penalty – check your scorecard for local rules. When you've played, leave the bunker as you'd wish to find it – litter free, raked and smooth.

CIGARETTE ENDS
You can move cigarette ends, sweet wrappers and the like – they're man-made objects.

FOOTPRINTS
You must play from footprints even though your ball can plug in them. Unfortunately you're paying for the lack of etiquette shown by another player.

RAKE MARKS
The ridges of sand created by the rake effectively plug your ball, but you can't claim anything under the rules.

LEAVES
If a stray leaf is lying next to your ball, you can't move it because the leaf is a natural object.

Putting

Almost half your shots in any round are putts so it is vital to develop a good stroke. If you putt well you are halfway to recording a decent score. Good putting is so important that just a handful of missed putts per round can mean the difference between a 19 and a 24 handicap.

The object of every putt is to hole the ball. If you don't, try to ensure that the ball is past the hole but near enough so that your next shot is from close range. Anything more than two putts per green is a waste of strokes.

After hitting tee and fairway shots 200yd (182m) or more, you finish every hole by putting the ball into the cup. Putts vary in distance from a 90ft (27m) one from the edge of a large green to a mere

tap-in from the edge of the hole. However, most putts are between 2-30ft (0.5-9m).

Because a putt is normally quite short, it needs the shortest swing and least energy of any shot. Yet good putting requires precise stroke-making.

ROLLING THE BALL

Putting requires a unique technique – rolling the ball along the ground. It is the only shot where the ball does not travel through the air. The ball travels over a special surface – the green – and you use a specially designed club – the putter.

The putter has the least loft of any club – between 2° and 4° – so you cannot use it for gaining height on the ball. It is also the shortest club in the bag and the most up-right. It has a small club-head and is not built for distance.

Head start
You should keep your head still while you putt. You can practise this indoors, by resting your head against a wall while putting on a carpet. Stand close to the wall and touch it gently with your head. Keep your head there so it can't move as you putt along the side of the wall.

PUTT IT RIGHT

Although the putting stroke is the shortest of all, it is vital to get it right. Stand parallel to the line of the putt with your left eye directly over the ball. The clubhead travels along this same line for most of the stroke.

Your shoulders, hips and toes are parallel to the line of the putt.

LEFT EYE OVER BALL

STANCE PARALLEL TO LINE OF PUTT

LINE OF THE PUTT

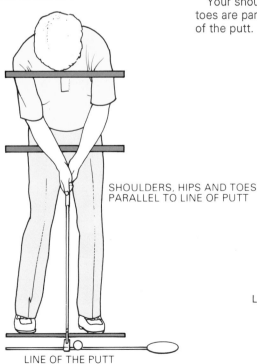

SHOULDERS, HIPS AND TOES
PARALLEL TO LINE OF PUTT

LINE OF THE PUTT

GETTING TO GRIPS

1 PLACE LEFT HAND ON GRIP
Leaving a gap at the top, grip the club lightly with the middle, third and little fingers of your left hand. Point your forefinger down the shaft and hold your thumb above the flat front side.

2 ADD RIGHT HAND
Slide the little, third and middle fingers of your right hand against your middle left finger. Rest your left thumb against the centre of the shaft. Point both forefingers down the shaft.

3 COMPLETE THE GRIP
Wrap the forefinger of your right hand round the grip and rest your right thumb down the shaft. Let your left forefinger lie across your right hand. A straight line runs through wrist, hand and shaft.

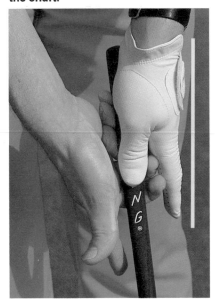
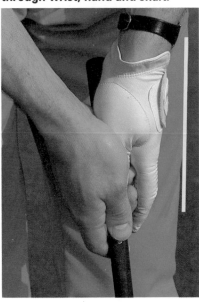

THE PUTTING STROKE

1 YOUR ADDRESS POSITION
The ball is opposite the inside of your left heel and your left eye is directly over the ball. Stand parallel to the line of the putt.

2 THE BACKSTROKE
Take the clubhead back straight. Your hands, arms and shoulders form one unit – a triangle which moves but never changes shape. Keep your head and lower body still.

LINE OF THE PUTT

Before you make your stroke you must decide on the line of the putt. This is not necessarily a straight line between ball and target – the ball-to-target line – because the roll of the ball will be affected by slopes.

To find the line of the putt try to visualize the path of your ball between its start position and the hole. If the green slopes from left down to right, the ball travels in the same direction, so compensate by selecting a point left of the hole at which to aim your putt. A straight line between the ball and this imaginary hole is called the line of the putt. A ball putted towards the imaginary hole curves with the slope and into the actual hole.

The exact point at which you aim depends on the severity of the slope and the length of the shot. The longer the putt and the greater the slope, the further away from the actual hole you should aim. This is because the more extreme conditions make the ball break further from the original line of the putt.

As well as assessing cross-slopes, you must take into account up and down slopes. An uphill putt needs a firmer strike than a downhill stroke.

Much of visualization is common sense, but to be really good at it requires practice and experience. The more you putt, the easier you'll find it to judge the pace and direction.

AIM AND GRIP

Once you have established the line of the putt, aim the clubface square on to it. Some putters have a mark on the clubhead to help you aim correctly. Then you take up your grip.

There are almost as many putting grips as there are individual players but the reverse overlap is the most popular putting grip in today's game. It is similar to the standard overlap grip, with one difference: the forefinger of the left

3 THROUGH IMPACT
The throughstroke follows the same straight line as the backstroke. Keep your left wrist firm through impact to ensure the clubhead is pulled smoothly through the ball.

4 ENDING THE STROKE
The clubhead continues to the same height as the top of the backstroke. Your hands, arms and shoulders still move as one. Let your head rotate slightly to the left after impact.

hand changes places with the little finger of the right hand. This change helps to keep your left hand, arm and shoulder moving correctly through the ball.

POSTURE AND ALIGNMENT

The key point about putting posture is that you stand so that your eyes are directly over the ball at address. This gives you a clear view of the line of the putt and makes aiming easier. It usually means that you have to stand with your knees slightly bent and your back bent from the waist.

Because the putter is the shortest, most upright, club in the bag you stand close to the ball. With your feet about 12in (30cm) apart, stand so that the ball is opposite the inside of your left heel. By placing the ball forward in your stance you hit it on the upstroke. This produces topspin and gives a consistent roll. Your weight is evenly spread throughout.

As with all golf strokes, alignment is crucial. when putting you align your feet, knees, hips and shoulders parallel to line of putt.

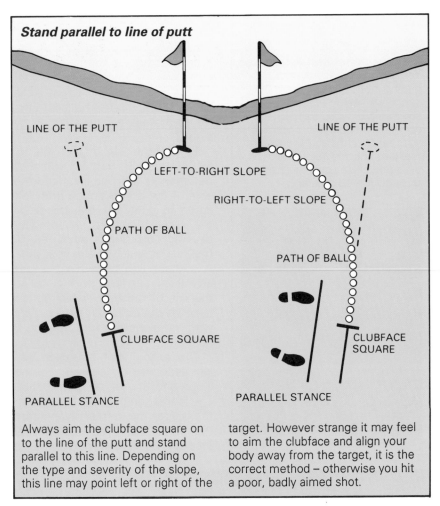

Stand parallel to line of putt

LINE OF THE PUTT

LINE OF THE PUTT

LEFT-TO-RIGHT SLOPE

RIGHT-TO-LEFT SLOPE

PATH OF BALL

PATH OF BALL

CLUBFACE SQUARE

CLUBFACE SQUARE

PARALLEL STANCE

PARALLEL STANCE

Always aim the clubface square on to the line of the putt and stand parallel to this line. Depending on the type and severity of the slope, this line may point left or right of the target. However strange it may feel to aim the clubface and align your body away from the target, it is the correct method – otherwise you hit a poor, badly aimed shot.

Judging pace and distance

To help you develop a feel for length, practise this simple routine. Place five balls in a line at 12in (30cm) intervals from the hole. Starting with the one nearest the hole, try to sink each ball in turn.

For each putt set yourself up carefully and assess the length of the stroke. Repeat until your back and throughstrokes are automatically the correct length to hole the ball.

THE STROKE

The putting stroke is dictated by your hands, arms and shoulders – which move as one unit. There is no body rotation, unlike full iron and wood shots. This is why it is vital to align your shoulders correctly at address.

Take the clubhead back with your hands, arms and shoulders moving together. The length of the backstroke is determined by the length of the putt. The clubhead travels in a straight line for most of the stroke, and only briefly moves inside the line of the putt as it nears the top of the backstroke.

Follow the same path into impact, keeping your left wrist firm. This allows the clubhead to be pulled through the ball on the correct line and prevents your right hand from flicking at it. Accelerate the clubhead through impact. Keep your head and lower body still, while allowing the clubhead to swing in a pendulum motion. The back and throughstrokes are of equal length.

Long putts

any golfers spend hours on the practice range trying to improve their wood and long iron play – but neglect their putting stroke. That's why putting is the most underrated part of the game – but you strike almost half your shots on the green.

You shouldn't take more than two putts on any green. Yet most players waste more shots here than anywhere else on the course. A 3 putt is damaging to your confidence as well as your score – usually it's the result of a poor first putt. It's vital to work on a repeat-

PUTT TO A LARGER TARGET
When faced with a long putt try to roll your ball into an imaginary 3-4ft (1-1.5m) circle around the hole. Don't attempt to sink the shot. By setting an easier target you stand more chance of getting the ball close to the pin – expecting to hole it increases the pressure on you. If you try to sink a long putt you focus your attention on the hole rather than the stroke needed to combat the speed and slopes of the green. Widening the target is a psychological trick that works.

THE PENDULUM ACTION

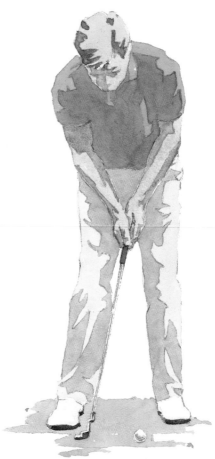

1 BALL OPPOSITE INSIDE OF LEFT HEEL
Stand with the ball opposite the inside of your left heel and your left eye directly over the ball. Your address position must be relaxed. Use the reverse overlap grip to help your feel for the shot.

2 SQUARE CLUBFACE
Keep the sole of the clubhead close to the ground for the first 12in (30cm) of the takeaway. To create the pendulum action of hands, arms and shoulders, keep the clubface and the back of your left hand square to the line of the putt for as long as possible on the backswing.

Late strike for smooth roll
For an even roll, place the ball opposite the inside of your left heel. Impact occurs late – on the upstroke – with the clubhead smoothly striking the ball forward.

If the ball is central in your stance impact is at the lowest point of the stroke. The clubhead hits down on the ball, pressing it slightly into the ground and causing it to bobble off line.

able putting stroke so that you can putt well from long distances.

Putting is the one area of the game where the high handicapper can perform as well as the low handicapper. This is because the stroke doesn't rely on power or an athletic swing. You can even practise putting in your own home.

Long putts are precision strokes. You must develop feel, intense concentration and an ability to read the green correctly.

ROLL THE BALL CLOSE

Although many players try to sink every putt – whatever the distance from the hole – they fail to hole most putts over 20ft (6m). This is true of even the most legendary players.

From beyond this distance you should try to stop your ball within 3ft (1m) of the hole. Don't expect

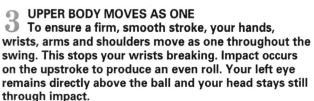

3 UPPER BODY MOVES AS ONE
To ensure a firm, smooth stroke, your hands, wrists, arms and shoulders move as one throughout the swing. This stops your wrists breaking. Impact occurs on the upstroke to produce an even roll. Your left eye remains directly above the ball and your head stays still through impact.

4 KEEP YOUR HEAD STILL
Even as the clubhead lifts up on the followthrough the clubface stays square to the line of the putt. As you complete the stroke – and not before – your head turns to face the hole. Your backswing and followthrough should be of equal length.

to sink it – if you hole a long putt accept it as a bonus. When you're a lengthy distance from the hole it's more important that you don't take 3 to get down.

READING THE GREEN

To assess your stroke accurately you must analyse two factors – the speed of the green and the lie of the land. Never be complacent – no two greens are the same.

Green speeds vary from course to course, season to season and at times even hole to hole. This happens for many reasons – mainly the soil type, its drainage and the type and length of the grass. The weather conditions are also important.

Bear in mind that the faster the green the more precisely you need to judge the speed and line of a putt, as the ball breaks more acutely on fast greens.

You must also assess the lie of the land between your ball and the hole. The slope of the green affects the line of the putt. Will the ball travel straight or curve left to right?

SPEED AND LINE

The steeper the slope the greater the curve and further left or right of the hole you must aim.

To putt well, both speed and slope must be judged correctly. Checking for slopes is fairly obvious to the eye, but speed is a mixture of experience and trial and error. Most 3 putts are caused by misjudging the pace. Try to get a feel for pace early in your round and learn from it.

For longer putts, assessing speed is more important than gauging the line as distance from the hole gets bigger. This is because there is less margin for error over long

distances.

You should not be more than 3ft (1m) off line from wherever you putt. A slight miscalculation in pace can result in your ball finishing 10-12ft (3-4m) away. Some greens are so fast that even the smallest boost in putter head speed means a difference of 10-15 ft (3-5m).

To become an accurate long putter you must combine correct green reading with a repeatable stroke.

REVERSE OVERLAP GRIP

Remember that the putting grip is similar to the standard overlapping grip – with one small difference. The forefinger of your left hand rests along two fingers of your right hand. This reverse overlap grip gives you greater feel and reduces the chances of left wrist break.

MOVE AS ONE

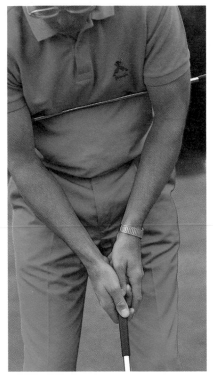

1 BACKSWING
Hold a club lengthways between your chest and upper arms before adopting your putting stance and starting your backswing.

Take an open stance – it helps you to see the line – and make sure your hands are square to the line of the putt. The ball should be opposite the inside of your left heel. This is slightly further forward in your stance than normal.

2 IMPACT
The club under your arms forces your shoulders, hands and arms to move as one unit through impact – if they don't, you drop the club.

Impact occurs later than usual – on the upstroke – to help produce a smooth, even roll.

Stand with your left eye over the ball. This lets you look directly along the line of the putt. If it feels uncomfortable, your putter must

3 THROUGHSWING
Your hands are still passive as your upper body – which moves as one unit throughout – completes the throughswing.

be either too long or too short for your height and needs changing.

Aim the clubface square to the line of the putt. Take the club a way with both hands – everything must work together – keeping the back of your left hand and the clubface square to the line of the putt. Keep the sole of the clubhead close to the ground, without letting it touch.

PENDULUM ACTION

Imagine the clubhead as a pendulum – moving back and through impact on the same line. Your hands should be passive – let your hands, wrists, arms and shoulders move as one to create a smooth, unhurried stroke.

The length of the putt determines how far back you take the clubhead. The backswing and throughswing should be the same length. This promotes even clubhead speed as you swing through. Don't speed up or slow down the club through impact – it affects the putt's pace.

Practise your putting regularly to develop a consistent technique and a feel for the shot.

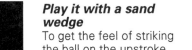

Play it with a sand wedge
To get the feel of striking the ball on the upstroke, practise putting with a sand wedge. With the ball opposite the inside of your left heel, try to strike so that the leading clubface edge makes contact with the middle of the ball.

Unless impact is perfect, the ball jumps and bobbles towards the hole. Only when the roll is smooth and even is your putting stroke correct. Don't practise this on the course – you should not take divots on the green.

Steep slope putting

Judging pace is critical if you are to avoid three putting on steeply sloping greens. But a fine judgement of speed must be linked with good reading of the line. The pace determines the line. You must first gauge the weight of the putt, then concentrate on the line and balance the two considerations.

DIFFERING APPROACHES

Aim to hole your first putt only when it's close to the pin. From long range think of two putting, as three putts are always a danger and holing out must be seen as a bonus.

Straight uphill: This is easily the simplest putt on a steeply sloping green. You can afford to hit the ball firmly and it still should drop because of the angle of the hole.

But be wary of overhitting the ball on a long putt – you could leave yourself a very awkward downhill putt.

From short range, make a smooth stroke and hit the ball firmly at the back of the hole.

Straight downhill: The pace is all important. Any putt going at even slightly more than perfect speed has little chance of dropping.

To help you judge the pace from long range, pick a point – perhaps an old hole or small mark on the green – between you and the hole. Choose a spot just a few inches away on a very steep green. Then play a normal putt to your spot – the slope carries the ball the rest of the way.

Always make sure you hit the ball with enough pace to send it past the hole should you miss. A

putt from 6ft (2m) straight back up the hill is far better than facing a tricky downhiller of 3ft (1m).

From short range concentrate on the line. Take time to set the blade exactly square to the target line because a downhill putt that catches the lip spins out unless going very slowly. Never leave a putt short from close range – it's a waste of a stroke.

Long putt across the slope: The ideal putt across a steep green is for the ball to topple in from the

EXPLORE ALL ANGLES
There is an art to balancing the line and pace on a steeply sloping green – an understanding of how the ball behaves from all angles makes putting much easier. From long range aim to knock your ball just past the hole to leave an uphill second. Holing out is a bonus.

top side. For this you judge the weight of the shot so the ball comes almost to a standstill above but nearly level with the hole. The ball then rolls down the slope and comes in from almost 90°.

But be realistic – aim to two putt on most occasions. Your main thought should be to lag the ball and regard holing out first time as a bonus.

Pace and line are vital. If you under or overhit the ball – even if you've chosen a good line – you're left with the same awkward type of putt but from a slightly shorter distance. Hit the ball too low and it gathers speed down the slope and runs well by. Hit too high and

the ball stays up on the top side and you're left with a tricky downhill breaking putt.

Short putt across the slope: Aim at a point level with the hole. Again almost stop the ball on the top side so that it rolls slowly down towards the hole.

Always allow more break than you think – it's better to be on the top side (known as the pro side) because the ball has a chance of dropping in as it trickles slowly down the hill. Once the ball falls below the line of the hole it can't break back up the hill.

Die the ball into the hole rather than play an aggressive stroke. This eliminates any risk of the putt

lipping out and running away down the slope.

Combination putt: When you're faced with a putt across the slope, but also either up or down the green, there is one vital point to bear in mind. The slower the ball is travelling the more it breaks.

A downhill putt across a slope needs to be given a much wider berth than an uphill putt with the same amount of break.

A downhiller has to played with caution – unless it's definitely holeable be content to two putt. An uphill putt can be hit firmly on a narrow line – the ball breaks near the hole, and you can afford to be aggressive.

pro tip

Toe tip
An excellent way to gain more control over a downhill putt is to hit the ball off the toe of the putter. This deadens the strike – the ball doesn't come off the clubface as fast as it would if struck in the middle of the blade.

It's especially useful when you need just to set the ball rolling on a very steep slope or down lightning fast greens.

Pace pointer
If you find difficulty in judging the pace of a downhill putt – particularly with break – hit a normal putt at a chosen point between you and the hole. It may be an old hole, a small leaf or patch on the green.

If you have judged the slope properly the ball is carried past this point and breaks naturally down towards the hole. The faster the putt the nearer your imaginary point should be.

This method helps you focus on your putting stroke rather than worrying about the putt itself.

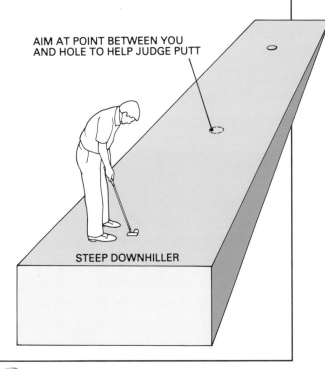

AIM AT POINT BETWEEN YOU AND HOLE TO HELP JUDGE PUTT

STEEP DOWNHILLER

masterclass

The Crenshaw touch
Ben Crenshaw is regarded by his fellow pros as one of the greatest putters of modern times. He combines a rock solid stroke with his natural ability to read greens. The American's understanding of how a steeply sloping green affects putts has helped him gain this reputation.

Crenshaw accurately judges the pace and line of even the fastest and most steeply sloping greens. His touch was at its best when he conquered the world's hardest greens at Augusta and won the 1984 Masters.

Holing six footers

Being able to hole out consistently from the awkward range of about 6ft (1.8m) is vital for good scoring. It's a confidence booster to know that even if you miss the green and your chip finishes that tricky distance away you have a very good chance of saving par.

Problems with this shot are mainly mental – a negative attitude can hinder your technique. The length of swing is so short that it's hard for a proper technique to go drastically wrong on its own.

STRAIGHT BACK

Although the club naturally moves inside the line on the backswing of a long putt, the path should be almost straight back along the ball-to-target line on a short putt. There is only a very slight move inside – if at all – on a six footer.

The crucial points are at impact and the followthrough. The blade should always return square at impact, and you must follow through along the ball-to-target line on a straight putt. This reduces the risk of pushing or pulling the ball and missing the putt.

If you swing a putter along the target line on a straight putt, only the pace or a bad kick can keep the ball out. Your stance should be sturdy but relaxed, and your action free of tension and smooth

CONFIDENCE AND TECHNIQUE
Six footers are awkward. While you expect to hole a short putt, and finding the cup from afar is a bonus, holing out from about a flag's length away is puttable – just. Be bold – all you need is confidence and a sound technique.

SIX FOOTER SUCCESS

1 TARGET LINE TAKEAWAY
Your takeaway must be smooth with no wrist break – you should be conscious of the club moving back along the ball-to-target line. The clubhead moves naturally inside on the backswing (below), but the movement should be only very slight.

2 DOWN THE LINE
The blade must be square at impact. Make sure the club follows through along the target line – it mustn't move to the inside. The proper line keeps the clubface square to the target for as long as possible, reducing the risk of a pull or a push.

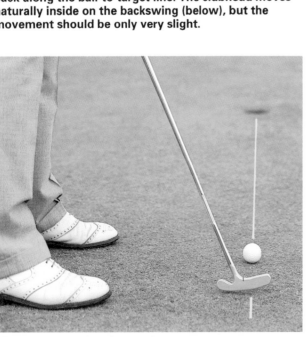

3 CONTROLLED FINISH
Hold the club at the finish position. Resist the tendency to jerk the putter back to the address position after impact – this leads to a jabbing stroke. Notice how the head has remained still throughout the stroke. Don't look up until you hear the putt drop, or your body can turn at impact and pull the ball off line.

yet controlled. Keep your grip light, and make sure you never break your wrists.

Stay perfectly still throughout the stroke. To help you achieve this, never look up to watch the ball rolling towards the hole. Wait until you hear the putt drop. This helps keep the putter swinging on the proper path.

On a breaking putt the technique remains the same but you must now judge the line and pace carefully. Don't be tempted to guide the ball at the hole – once you have chosen your line, putt straight along it letting the slope – not your putter blade – turn the ball back towards the target.

Confidence is the key – build it up by going out to practice. A positive attitude helps you relax and make a good stroke when it matters. Having negative thoughts on the greens can destroy even the best putting technique. Always try to be positive and assume you're going to hole out every six footer.

pro tip

Eye drops
It is a great help to be able to turn your head while standing over a putt to see straight down the line to the hole. For this your eyes should be directly over the ball. To find the position, hold a ball on the bridge of your nose and then drop it. Where the ball lands is where you should place it in your stance.

EYES OVER BALL

pro tip

Tee peg training

Placing two sets of tee pegs in the practice green to channel your club is an excellent way to ingrain the proper stroke into your game. The sets should be about 10in (25cm) apart, and just wide enough for your clubhead to pass through.

Place a ball in the middle of the rectangle formed by the tees. Swing the putter away and through the back two pegs without touching either one. Hitting a peg means you have taken the club away on the wrong line.

Swing through smoothly making sure the putter blade travels between the front tees. This ensures the blade follows through along the target line.

Hold the finish position. Notice how a straight line can be drawn from the centre of the rectangle through clubhead, ball and to the hole.

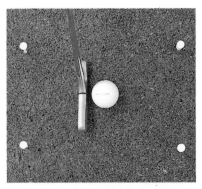

masterclass

Fearless Faldo

Double Open champion Nick Faldo is cool under pressure and expects to hole six footers. Because his technique is excellent – straight back and through – and his temperament ideal, the awkward length putt holds no fear for him. With an extremely smooth and confident stroke he misses very few putts of a flag's length.

Faldo's stroke held up under the severest of pressure from about 5ft (1.5m) in the final round of the 1987 Open at Muirfield. He had to hole out several times from this tricky length to save his par. Incredibly, the man from Hertfordshire parred all 18 holes – at the last, this missable one clinched the title.

Charge or die putting

To achieve a consistent putting game on sloping greens, it is important to know when to attack and when to defend. A firmly struck, aggressive putt aimed at the back of the hole is called a charge. For a die putt you need a more calculating, cautious approach – the aim being to roll the ball gently up to the hole so it just topples into the cup.

Your technique for hitting either a charge or die putt remains exactly the same as normal. The difference between the shots is how firmly the putt is struck and the line taken. Across a slope, a charge putt travels to the hole along a straighter path than a die, which is given a wider berth.

As you hit the charge putt fairly straight, you must also strike the ball firmly to counter the effect of the slope. You have to hit a die putt on a wider line because it needs a softer strike, so the slope has more time to affect the ball's path.

AGGRESSION OR DEFENCE

The perfect time to hit a charge putt is on an uphill slope – even if the ball breaks. Coming down the green across the same slope, hit a die putt to limit the risk of the ball racing past the hole if you miss.

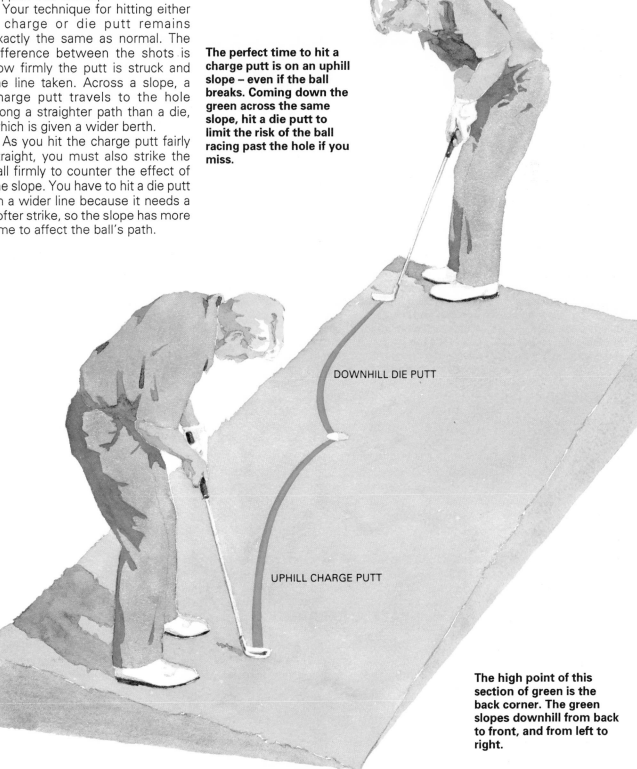

DOWNHILL DIE PUTT

UPHILL CHARGE PUTT

The high point of this section of green is the back corner. The green slopes downhill from back to front, and from left to right.

SPEED AND LINE

LEFT-TO-RIGHT SLOPE

FAST GREEN
DIE PUTT

NORMAL SPEED

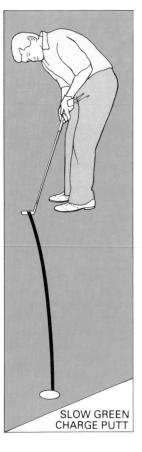

SLOW GREEN
CHARGE PUTT

SLICK GREEN
When a green has been newly mown for a competition it's usually very fast. You should give the ball more width and try to die the ball into the hole, reducing the risk of three putting.

MEDIUM PACED
On the same-sloped green of normal speed your decision to charge or die depends on how confident you feel, and whether you need to attack or defend your score. It's foolish to charge if a two putt wins you the hole.

SLOW AND GRASSY
When the same green hasn't been cut for a few days and is slow, the ball doesn't break as much as normal so you can afford to charge most of your putts. Even if you miss, the ball shouldn't run too far by.

Palmer's charging
In his heyday one of the great trademarks of Arnold Palmer's game was the way he used to attack the hole with his putts. He was never afraid of aiming for the back of the hole and giving the ball a good rap. Even if he missed, he was such a fine putter that the return was always holeable. The famous Palmer charging putts helped him win seven major titles.

DO OR DIE

The decision whether to play a charge or die comes with experience. Think about the slope, the state of play and the speed of the green.

Slope: Any uphill putt is a potential charge. You can afford to be bold with the shot if you know that – should you miss – the ball would not go too far past. But there is little point in charging a downhill putt, because if you miss the ball rolls well past the hole. One downhill exception is when the green is so slow that the ball can't go too far past the hole.

Hit the die instead of the charge if you have to putt across a very steep slope. A charge gathers pace on the slope and unless you hole out the ball runs by.

State of play: You can take an aggressive approach to a downhill putt if you need a birdie to avoid losing a hole or the match. But there is no point in hitting a charge when you have the luxury of two putts to win a hole or competition, even if it's uphill. Be content to take the two putts by dying the ball at the hole.

Speed: When a green is lightning fast you should aim to die the ball at the hole. On a very slow green you can charge most putts unless it's severely downhill.

PACE AND PRACTICE

Whatever your choice, judging the pace of the putt is all important. Knowing how firmly to hit a putt along different lines comes with experience. You should experiment on the practice putting green.

For both types of putt you must pick a spot to aim at. With a die putt it's best to pinpoint a spot you want the ball to roll over between you and the hole. With a charge, choose a point level with the hole and aim to hit the ball at it. If you read the break properly the ball hits the back of the hole and drops in.

When you're deciding how hard and how wide you need to hit the ball towards the hole, it's essential to visualize the path and how the slope affects it.

Being able to weigh up the facts quickly and make the right decision on the putting green – do you want to charge or die? – is vital to protect your score. Often it's a decision that must be made under pressure in a match – prepare yourself by brushing up these putting skills.

Perfect your putting

It's the most talked and written about aspect of golf, and it's often the most frustrating. None of this is pure coincidence – putting is the most crucial area in any round of golf.

A look at the 1990 European Tour statistics is proof in itself. Bernhard Langer averaged less than 29 putts per round having played in 17 tournaments and finished fourth in the Order of Merit with prize money of over £420,000.

The putting stroke requires less movement than any other shot – yet a sound technique on the greens eludes golfers the world over. Lack of ability is rarely to blame – not enough practice is often the culprit.

There are endless opportunities to practise your putting. You don't need much space and you can putt indoors as well as outdoors – even if it's only putting to a chair leg.

Whether it's on the carpet or on

STATISTICAL EVIDENCE
When you're next in a competition at your home club, talk to a golfer with a good score – he's likely to be someone who putted well. When that happens, every long putt tends to finish close and the short ones drop with monotonous regularity. It's seldom down to luck – hard work on the practice putting green is usually the only way to achieve this type of success.

A FEEL FOR DISTANCE

1 COMFORTABLE ADDRESS
Above all you must feel comfortable and relaxed at address on the greens. Think of grip pressure – it must remain consistent throughout the stroke. Check the alignment of the putter head – it should be square to the line you want the ball to roll along.

2 INSIDE TAKEAWAY
On a longish putt, sweep the putter back slightly inside the ball-to-target line. The distance you are from the hole determines the length of your backswing. Whatever style of putting stroke you adopt, there should be no movement from the waist down.

pro tip

Trial and error
Every golfer loses confidence on the greens from time to time – it usually only needs a couple of putts to drop for your state of mind to be transformed. But sometimes it pays to search for an alternative cure.

Most club professionals are happy to let you on to the practice green with a variety of putters. The face is usually taped up for protection, but you soon develop an overall feel for the club.

Take about half a dozen balls and stroke putts across the green swapping different clubs. It doesn't take long to discover which of the putters you like and which are totally unsuitable.

More often than not, practising with a variety of putters makes you realize that the old faithful you were about to dispense with is not quite as bad as you thought. Either way, you stand an excellent chance of restoring lost confidence.

3 RETURN TO SQUARE
With a fundamentally sound putting stroke the position at impact mirrors that at address. The putter face returns square to the ball with the hands leading the clubhead through impact. Strike the ball slightly on the up to generate the necessary overspin.

4 SET THE PACE
Smoothly accelerate the putter head through impact – it should travel slightly inside the line again to complete the in-to-in path of the clubhead. Only now should you look up. Repeat the same putt several times to test your ability to judge pace consistently.

the putting green, there's just one factor that should remain the same – always introduce variety into your practice to ensure your interest level remains high.

FREEDOM OF CHOICE

There's no right or wrong way to putt – it's very much a case of finding a system that works for you. Nick Faldo is a shoulders and arms putter. Gary Player has a wristy, stabbing type putting stroke. The only similarity is that their techniques are awesomely effective.

There are certain fundamentals which are consistent with most great putters – hands directly above the ball at address; a constant grip pressure throughout the stroke and the putter blade square to the intended line.

Once you have a comfortable style based on sound technique, the next step is to build into your game a method that works over and over again even under severe pressure. The practice putting green is the place to groove a repeatable stroke.

Place several balls in a circle around a hole to sharpen your short range putts. Attempt to knock in each ball and only move on to another drill when each one is in the hole. If you miss one, start all over again – this adds an exciting element of pressure into the exercise.

To improve your feel for distance, stroke a ball from one side of the putting green to the other. Then attempt to stop another dozen balls on precisely the same spot – the tighter the grouping

the better your judgment of line and weight.

COMPETITIVE EDGE

It's always a good idea to set aside a few minutes for pre-round preparation, particularly if you're in a competition.

An excellent way to brush up on your stroke is to hit several long putts. Concentrate on making a smooth swing – note how the ball comes off the putter face. You should be looking to sharpen your judgment of distance.

It's seldom advisable to practise short putts just before a competitive round. It only needs a couple to slip by the hole and your confidence takes a dive. This is unlikely to have you stepping on to the 1st green in a very positive frame of mind.

Always use the same ball on the practice putting green as you would on the course. Don't carelessly pluck a two piece solid ball from your bag if you intend playing a balata out on the course. The difference in feel between the two is enormous.

COPY SLAMMIN' SAM

As soon as you walk on to the 1st green, take a close look at the length and texture of the grass. It may differ slightly from the type found on the practice green and have an effect on the roll of your ball.

If you find you're having a bad day on the greens – and it happens to everyone from time to time – try adopting the Sam Snead philosophy. He was once quoted as saying about short putts, 'if you're going to miss one, miss it quick'. You may be pleasantly surprised – a carefree approach might make the putts start to drop again.

Blind spot
Putting is such a precision art that it's easy to tie yourself up in knots over technique. Do you crouch over the ball or stand upright? Is an open or square stance best? How do you grip the club? The permutations are seemingly endless.

Sometimes it's a good idea to forget about the text book and rely solely on feel. Putting with your eyes closed can help you achieve this – it relieves tension in your body and places the emphasis on your stroke.

Address the ball with your eyes open. When you feel comfortable, close your eyes and putt the ball towards the hole. Before you open them again, try to predict where the ball has finished – short or long, pulled left, pushed right or dead straight.This exercise increases your control over the putter head and develops your feel for line and length on the greens.

Listen – don't look
One of the keys to Nick Faldo's 1990 Open victory at St Andrews was his impeccable holing out. His only 3 putt of the entire championship was from long range at the treacherous Road hole. That was in the final round and by then the tournament was his.

Copying a technique practised by Nick Faldo may help you to hole out more regularly – but it's something you need to experiment with on the practice putting green before you carry it out in a competition.

On short putts wait for the sound of the ball dropping into the hole before you look up. This encourages you to concentrate on the stroke rather than ball direction.

Looking up before striking the ball causes miss-hits and is one of the major causes of missing short putts.

Playing in the rain

Few golfers relish the prospect of playing in the rain. Wet weather affects the playing conditions of the course, and may lower morale – there's nothing more miserable than struggling through a round feeling the damp seep through clothes and shoes.

But with careful planning, playing in the rain needn't be a washout. To play your best, learn to adapt your game with a few simple techniques, and always set out properly equipped for a sudden shower.

Modern wet-weather clothing is light and waterproof, and does much to keep you comfortably dry. Buy the best you can afford, and look after it carefully, so that you continue to enjoy your game whatever the weather. Have it with you whenever you play a round.

READY FOR THE RAIN

A few well chosen wet-weather basics should give good service for years.

A men's golf **umbrella** is larger and stronger than a normal one. For extra protection on an exposed course, choose one with a sturdy frame – a weak-framed umbrella is likely to collapse when the wind picks up.

There's a smaller golf umbrella for women and junior players which is robust and easy to hold on to in high winds.

Keep two large **towels** in your bag. Use one to dry and clean your clubface before and after every shot. Grass, mud and water clog up the grooves so that you don't make firm contact with the ball at impact, and your control over

the shot is reduced.

Dry and clean your ball on the same towel after every hole and before you putt.

You can't lift and clean the ball between the tee and the green, so when you're playing from a wet fairway there's likely to be water on the ball at impact. This reduces control and the amount of spin you put on the ball, which ends in a flier – the ball doesn't stop as quickly as it should on landing. Also, when you strike a wet ball a certain amount of spray is thrown

KEEP YOUR HANDS AND GRIPS DRY
Before every shot, dry your hands and the grip with a towel to give you a firm hold on the club. If either are wet the club is likely to slip in your hands – especially at impact.

Clean the clubhead for control

Always dry and clean the clubface before hitting the ball. Mud, grass or moisture that gets trapped between the clubface and the ball cushions the power, reducing length as well as control. You can waste shots needlessly if you try to ignore the problem.

Remove mud from spikes

To keep a firm footing on wet ground, check your spikes every few holes and remove mud and grass. If too much dirt builds up on the bottom of your shoes it stops the spikes digging into the ground and gripping on a slippery surface.

Secure your grip

Wear a rubber rain glove for a secure grip in the wet. Rubber gives a firmer hold than leather or any other material, and reduces the risk of the club slipping in your hands – which ruins your shot.

COPING WITH CASUAL WATER

IN THE BUNKER
If you land in a bunker area flooded with casual water you can lift and drop your ball on the nearest dry section without penalty – but the ball must stay in the same bunker.

ON THE GREEN
When your path to the pin is obstructed by an area of casual water you can place your ball on the nearest dry point the same distance away from the hole – the rules don't let you move closer to the hole.

Beware the flier
When playing a shot from wet rough you get even less backspin than if hitting from dry rough. Moisture trapped between the clubface and the ball stops the grooves making clean contact and imparting backspin. This creates a flier, with the ball running further than normal on landing.

When you visualize the shot, aim to land the ball shorter than you normally would to allow for the lack of backspin.

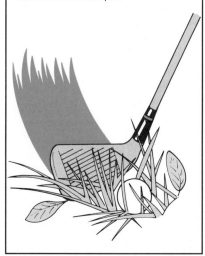

up, slowing the ball down as it travels through the air or along the ground.

Take the effects of water into account, and allow for less back-spin, when visualizing shots in the rain.

Use the second towel to dry your hands and the grip as thoroughly as possible. If they're wet the club is likely to slip in your hands during the swing, and the clubface won't strike the ball squarely.

KEEPING DRY

A good **waterproof suit** makes all the difference to a round in the rain – keep one in your bag at all times so you're always prepared for a sudden shower. The best type of wet-weather suit lets air pass through, keeping you cool and dry. Beware of buying a cheap airtight suit which traps the moisture in, leaving you hot and sticky.

As well as keeping your head dry, a peaked **golf hat** stops water running down your face. A hat makes for greater comfort and concentration – rain trickling down your face may blur your vision and put you off your shot.

A **rain glove** helps you grip a club firmly in the rain. This type of glove is made from rubber – it's similar to a washing-up glove. In damp conditions rubber gives a firmer hold than other materials, and stops the club from turning in your hands.

If it starts to rain during a round replace your normal glove with a rain glove immediately. Never use a leather glove in the rain. Not only is it more liable to slip in your grip, but moisture ruins the glove.

Keep your clubs dry under a waterproof **bag hood.** This stops water running down inside the bag and making your clubs wet. Most new bags have hoods, or you can buy one separately from some pro shops.

If you play most of your golf in a damp climate ask your club pro to fit your clubs with **half-cord grips**. This type of rubber grip fits over your regular grip to give a more secure hold when it rains.

Waterproof shoes, also made from rubber, stop water seeping through so you can avoid the dismal experience of playing a round with wet feet. For a firm footing in slippery conditions, check after every few holes that your studs aren't clogged up – remove excess mud and grass with a tee-peg.

SWINGING IN THE RAIN

As well as having the correct wet-weather equipment you must also be aware of swing problems caused by wet conditions.

A normal swing is difficult in a wet-weather suit. The extra weight and additional layers restrict body movement. Don't try to overcome the problem by forcing your swing. Keep your normal tempo and make a three-quarter swing if it feels easier.

The key is to maintain your concentration and tempo in the rain. This may be harder than you think. A wet fairway slows down the roll of the ball, so many players wrongly increase the speed of their swing to compensate for reduced length. This is often disastrous.

When the course plays long, take one more club than usual and concentrate on keeping the same tempo as always. It's particularly important to play within your limits in damp conditions. Never gamble.

KNOW THE RULES

It's vital to understand the rules that apply to rain-affected areas of the course.

Excessive rain can cause small areas of the green, fairway and bunker to become flooded. These areas are described as 'casual water' in the Royal and Ancient rules book.

If there's casual water directly between your ball and the pin when you're putting, you can re-position the ball – but not move it nearer the hole in the process.

If your ball lands in casual water you can lift it out and drop it on the nearest dry area without penalty. In a bunker the nearest point of relief must be in that same bunker – and not the nearest dry point on the fairway or green.

If you lose your ball in casual water you can drop another one without penalty near to the point where you think it landed – providing your partners agree. You pick up a 1-stroke penalty, as with a normal lost ball, if your partners don't agree that the ball finished in casual water.

STAY DRY IN A WATERPROOF SUIT
Wear a wet-weather suit in the rain. If you don't, your clothes become damp and uncomfortable which may upset your concentration.

Checklist
Be prepared for rain whenever you play a round. Keep wet-weather equipment in your golf bag at all times.
- You need a strong and sturdy umbrella, specially built to withstand high winds.
- Carry two towels – one to keep your clubface and ball dry, the other to dry your hands and grip.
- A bag hood stops water getting inside your bag and making the clubs wet.
- Made from rubber, a rain glove gives a firmer grip than leather in the wet.
- A good waterproof suit is light and keeps out the rain while letting air through.
- A peaked hat or cap stops water running down your face and into your eyes, which is uncomfortable and puts you off your stroke.

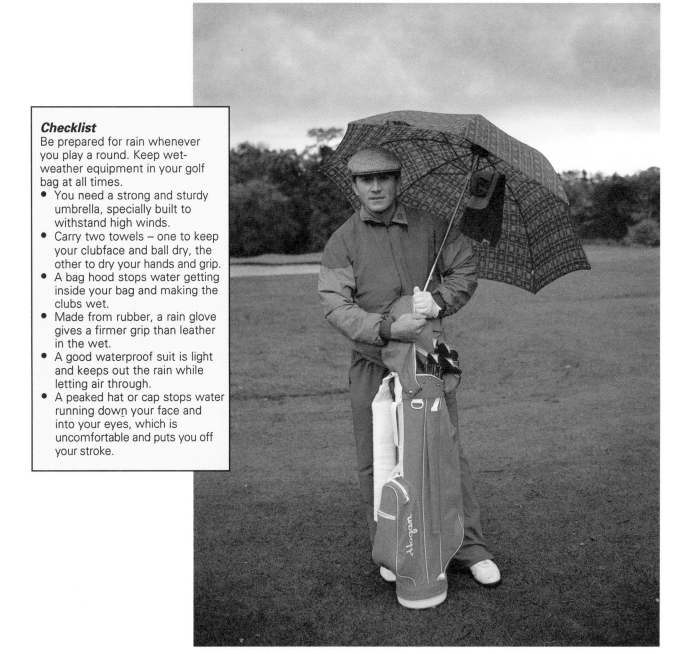

Playing a parkland course

Successfully making your way round a parkland course demands a particular approach to golf – it's not like playing any other type of course. The conditions are completely different from links and heathland – as are the hazards which confront you. The ground tends to be flat and there are always plenty of trees, so you must form your strategy accordingly.

Correct club selection is all important if you want to give yourself the best chance of hitting a good shot. Don't make life difficult for yourself. Learn to understand what clubs are best suited to certain situations.

Lush grass on the fairways can cause you to hit a flyer on any full shot. Grass comes between the clubface and ball at impact, so less spin is applied causing the ball to fly further than you might expect.

HARD OR SOFT

As well as being flat, parkland courses are usually built on a clay base. Drainage is always a problem and conditions vary from one extreme to the other.

In summer the ground is often very hard - let the ball run when you pitch. For the rest of the year it is usually soft with plenty of grass all over. Conditions in the winter months may become unpleasant underfoot with wet, muddy fairways and greens. The ball pitches and stops quickly wherever you hit it. In these conditions you can afford to be more forceful with your shots.

It's no use playing a links type pitch and run shot along winter parkland fairways. The ball simply comes up short. Instead, hit the ball high into the air and pitch it all the way on to the green.

PARKLAND SHOTS
Parkland fairways are soft except in high summer. When they're soft, hit a high approach shot that pitches all the way to the green. Where bunkers guard the flag, aim to the safe part of the green. If you learn to understand the conditions around you, you perform well on all types of golf course, not just your home club.

pro tip

Practise pitching

Encouraging good feel in your short game is a sure way to lower your scores out on the course. Feel for distance is something that cannot be taught though – it is achieved only through hard work.

Place a target – perhaps a towel or bag – about 50yd (45m) away and practise pitching balls to it with your wedge. Remember, greens on parkland courses are nearly always soft so aim to hit a high shot, landing the ball as near to the target as possible. If you make good contact the ball should stop quickly.

Go through this practice drill as often as you can.

CLUB SELECTION

Parkland grass is often quite lush. When your ball is sitting down in this type of grass and you are faced with a long shot, hit a wooden club. The clubhead slides through the grass for a better strike on the ball. An iron becomes tangled, causing the clubhead to twist at impact and the ball to fly off line.

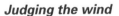

Judging the wind

It is difficult to judge the strength and direction of the wind on a parkland course – you tend to be sheltered by the trees. Throw grass high into the air and note which way it blows. Study the tree tops and clouds if you are still not sure. Play a low shot if it is very windy.

SUMMER SAFETY

Concentrate on accuracy off the tee in the summer. A drive that pitches and stops on soft winter fairways may run into trouble when the clay soil of parkland fairways is baked **hard. A lofted wood or long iron is the safer bet – length takes care of itself in dry conditions. Use a driver only when the fairway is wide.**

DRY SUMMER CONDITIONS

FAIRWAY WOOD
SAFE LESS ROLL

DRIVER IN TROUBLE
RUNS ON LANDING

What shoes to wear

✔ Think carefully about what shoes to wear before stepping out on to a damp, soggy golf course. Leather golf shoes with a manmade sole and spikes are good in wet conditions. They are comfortable and stop you from slipping around when you swing. Some rubber waterproof shoes are also excellent.

✗ Moulded studs provide very little grip in wet weather. In any case, many clubs ban them in winter because of the damage they cause to soft greens.

LOOSE OR LIVING

On a parkland course you come across many fluffy lies where there's fairly long grass around the ball. Think carefully before you move anything lying near. If something is growing, like the buttercups here, don't move it. This is a good maxim to keep you within the rules. You are allowed to move loose impediments – dead twigs or scraps of paper – but only if the lie of your ball is not improved.

Sculled shot

Bunker sand on a parkland course is often hard packed, making the splash shot impossible to play. The clubhead bounces off the sand into the back of the ball sending it shooting across the green – a sculled (thin) shot.

Nip the ball cleanly taking as little sand as possible with a pitching wedge instead of a sand wedge. The ball flies lower and runs further than a normal bunker shot, so consider where you want to pitch the ball.

Once you've decided on the shot to play, don't change your mind. Second thoughts in golf usually result in disaster.

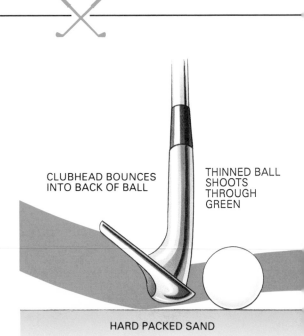

CLUBHEAD BOUNCES INTO BACK OF BALL

THINNED BALL SHOOTS THROUGH GREEN

HARD PACKED SAND

FAT SHOTS

The fat (heavy) shot happens when the clubhead makes contact with the turf before the ball. It's the most destructive shot you can hit in wet conditions if the ground is soft. You lose all clubhead speed and the ball travels no distance at all. When the ground is wet and spongy it's vital that you strike the ball cleanly.

HEAVY CONTACT LOSES DISTANCE

SOFT GROUND

Playing a heathland course

A combination of heather, gorse and tree lined fairways based on firm well drained soil makes heathland courses a delight to play. But don't be deceived by the beauty – danger lurks on every hole.

Heathland fairways aren't just skirted with trees – punishing heather and gorse bushes are ready to gather your ball. When you stray into heather it usually costs you at least a shot – all you can hope to do is hack out back on to the fairway.

Hit your ball into a gorse bush and the penalty is likely to be more severe. Forget trying to play a recovery shot – you'll be lucky if you can even retrieve your ball from the prickly branches.

HARD AND FAST

It's important when you tee up on a heathland course to think of accuracy more than distance. Your number one priority must be to keep the ball in play. You'll have the opportunity to hit irons off the tee for safety on a lot of holes, so brush up on your iron play if you're not confident with it.

The sandy well drained fairways can be used to good effect as they are invariably fast running. Your tee shots travel further so use a lofted wood or an iron if you're confident you can reach the green in regulation.

You often find yourself on bare, unforgiving lies on the closely mown fairways – it's essential you don't hit the ground before the ball. Grip the club slightly shorter to help you strike the ball cleanly with your iron shots. As an extra precaution, place the ball further towards the centre of your stance for clean contact.

PUNISHING IN PINK
Heather is an attractive feature of every heathland course but it's tough on your wrists. Many accomplished golfers come unstuck trying to do too much when they hit out of heather. If the ball is sitting down, play the shot with a wedge. Grip tightly to stop tangled heather closing the clubface at impact.

WOOD FROM HEATHER

1 FIRM GRIP
Risk an aggressive shot from heather only if you're confident the lie is good enough. Stand slightly closer to the ball and place it towards the centre of your stance – about the position you take with a mid iron. Grip more tightly than normal to prevent the clubhead twisting in the heather.

Splashing out
Greenside bunkers on a heathland course tend to be deep with soft sand – they are ideal for the high splash shot.

Open your stance so your shoulders, hips and feet align left of target – aim the clubface at the flag. Make a full backswing from out to in and pull the clubhead down with the left hand into the sand behind the ball. The clubhead cuts through the sand and the ball floats high, landing softly on the green.

2 UPRIGHT PLANE
Pick the club up more steeply on the backswing by breaking the wrists early in the swing. Your stance should help you swing on a more upright plane. Don't hit the ball hard out of the poor lie – maintain your control throughout the shot. Never go past horizontal at the top of the backswing.

3 STAY DOWN
Pull the butt of the club down with the back of the left hand – don't lunge forward with your upper body. The clubhead must strike the ball with a descending blow, cutting through the grass and heather. Watch the clubhead make contact with the ball to help you stay down on the shot through impact.

4 FREE FLOWING
The clubhead speed you generate at impact pulls your arms up into the followthrough position with your body facing the target. Your swing should flow freely at this stage. The control is maintained throughout the swing – there's no loss of balance as you watch the ball fly straight down the middle of the fairway.

Grass roots

All heathland courses have one advantage in common – firm, fast running fairways. The sandy soil is typical of heathland in damp climates such as in the UK. The ground drains extremely well which means you can play golf in firm conditions all year round. Very seldom is a heathland course damp and soggy.

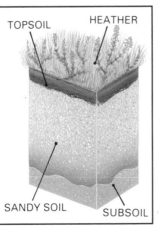

TOPSOIL   HEATHER

SANDY SOIL   SUBSOIL

ESCAPE TO SAFETY

From a poor lie in heather, reach for your wedge and look for the shortest route back to the fairway.

Don't ground the club – heather is springy and could move the ball, costing you a 1 stroke penalty. Grip

firmly, make a steep backswing and hit sharply down into the bottom of the ball.

SAND WEDGE TO SAFETY

pro tip

Sleeper shot
On many heathland courses railway sleepers are used to stop soil drift. For distance off a sleeper use a similar technique to a long bunker shot. Place the ball in the centre of your stance and grip well down. Make a three-quarter backswing and aim to nip the ball cleanly off the wooden surface. The ball flies low with almost no backspin and runs a long way. Take care – you might damage the clubhead and your wrists if you catch the shot heavy.

Use a mid iron to chip from a sleeper close to the green. Treat the shot very much like a long putt. Swing your arms back and through without breaking your wrists. Try to pitch the ball on the green so you can rely on a more even bounce.

THE RIGHT APPROACH

Let the course help you whenever possible. You don't have to pitch your approach shots on the green – particularly if you're playing downwind.

Look at the ground in front of you and assess what is the safest shot. With wise club selection you can achieve a good result without taking unnecessary risks. When the ground is hard use the natural contours of the fairway. Bounce the ball short of the target and let it run on to the green. A 5 iron may pitch all the way to the flag but most golf-

ers find a 7 iron is the easier club to hit straight.

WEATHER WATCH

Heathland courses are often situated on high ground and exposed to the elements. When it's windy let the breeze work for you – don't fight it.

Hitting a draw into a left to right wind is difficult and risky. Aim slightly left of target and let the wind bring the ball back on line. When you feel on top of your game try lower trajectory shots to keep the ball under the wind.

Playing a links

Links golf courses lie on often remote stretches of land close to the sea. Playing a links is an exhilarating but demanding experience. You're exposed to extreme weather conditions and usually play in winds far stronger than you ever experience inland.

From a distance such a course looks flat and quite featureless. But once you set foot on a links you discover that the ground is a mass of humps and hollows – many of the tee shots you face are semi-blind.

Hard, fast running fairways can cause the occasional unpredictable bounce. Your ball may shoot forward on the first bounce, while the same shot pitching into a hump stops quickly. If you're very unfortunate a ball flying straight down the middle of the fairway kicks into the rough.

The short grass and closely mown fairways on a links course can remove some of the fear from your mid range approach shots to the green. A crisply struck iron shot generates a great deal of backspin because very little grass comes between the clubface and the ball at impact.

WATCH THE WIND

Strong wind is an important feature of links golf, so make sure you use it to your advantage whenever possible. Try to forget the distance you usually hit the ball – wind drastically alters your normal club selection.

Into the wind demands a precise strike. Always take plenty of club and swing shorter than normal. A three-quarter shot helps you hit the ball lower to give you

TOTAL EXPOSURE
Links courses such as Troon in Scotland provide the purest, most natural form of golf in the world. Strong winds stretch every department of your game – you need control from the tee, accuracy with your irons and a delicate touch on undulating greens. An all round test for even the most accomplished golfer, links courses have staged the British Open since the first tournament in 1860.

PUNCHING LOW INTO WIND

1 SOLID AT ADDRESS
A bunker guards the flag so aim at the right edge of the green. Set up parallel to the target line with the ball central in your stance. Grip down and stand slightly closer to the ball than normal. Your left arm and the club shaft form a straight line.

2 CONTROLLED BACKSWING
Swing smoothly away from the ball, breaking the wrists halfway back. Concentrate on a full shoulder turn and stop the backswing short of horizontal – this helps you stay in complete control of the clubhead. The position at the top should feel solid and compact.

3 **SMOOTH DOWNSWING**
Gradually transfer your weight to the left on the downswing. Keep it smooth – many golfers mistakenly try to hit the ball harder into the wind. This only makes you swing more quickly and you risk losing control – remember the saying: don't hit it harder, hit it better.

4 **PURE STRIKE**
Keep your hands ahead of the ball at impact – if you scoop in the hitting area you rule out any hope of a low penetrating flight. The clubhead makes crisp contact first with the ball and then the turf. Notice how still the head remains until impact.

PUNCHING LOW THROUGH IMPACT

5 FLOWING FOLLOWTHROUGH
Allow your forearms to roll through impact. Stay down on the shot until you feel your arms pulling the body up into the followthrough position. Almost all of your weight is supported on the left foot – don't topple on to your right side or you miss-hit the shot.

6 PERFECT BALANCE
The swing looks and feels effortless. Clubhead speed has been generated by making the correct moves – not by sheer force and muscle power. The balance achieved earlier in the swing is maintained as you watch the ball fly quite low towards the green.

Fairway fallacy
Links fairways are undulating with lots of humps and hollows. They're also very fast running – a ball rolling on the fairway tends to be gathered in by the hollows.

You may have to cope with some wild bounces on a links, but the ball often finds level ground – you play from fewer uneven lies on the fairway than you might expect.

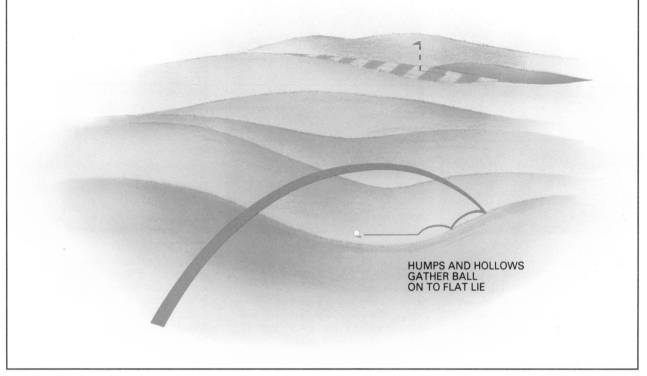

HUMPS AND HOLLOWS
GATHER BALL
ON TO FLAT LIE

pro tip

Better safe than sorry
Bunkers on a links are invariably deep – often the front edge is above head height. Even the best golfers can't play towards the flag from every bunker – as anyone who's watched top pros go through the 17th at St Andrews can testify.

Be content to escape from an awkward bunker away from the flag if necessary. Resist the temptation to try a miraculous recovery. You record fewer high scores on your card and playing a links becomes an enjoyable rather than frustrating experience.

more control in the wind.

Remember that playing into the wind exaggerates the spin off links turf and you can stop the ball even on firm greens.

Wind behind should encourage you to hit the ball higher to gain maximum distance on the shot. With luck you can reduce long par 5s to a comfortable 4 strokes and look for birdies on par 4s.

Downwind it's difficult to put enough backspin on the ball to pitch and stop it neatly on the green. Take less club, swing smoothly and let the wind carry the ball towards the target. Aim to pitch the ball well short of the green and expect plenty of run on the shot.

Cross winds force you to aim way off line and allow the ball to be blown back on target. Depending on the strength and direction of the wind, select a spot to one side and set up to hit the ball straight at it. Swing normally and let the wind do the rest.

SHORT GAME STRATEGY

Many golfers forget that wind affects the short game as well as the longer shots. This is especially true on a links course.

When you chip from close to the green your main thought must be to keep the ball near the ground. A low pitch and run is always a safer shot in wind than a high lob.

A 7 iron is the ideal club for the shot. The ball runs twice the distance it travels in the air, so select an area to pitch the ball on and visualize it running up towards the hole.

Grip down the club and position the ball towards the centre of your stance. Swing the club as you do with a long putt – the arms moving back and through together with very little wrist break. Make sure you keep your hands ahead of the ball throughout to promote a crisp strike.

Bear in mind that a long putt on a large sloping links green can often take two or three different breaks. It's important to study the slope of the green carefully. Look at a putt along the ball-to-target line and then from side on to give you a better perspective. Wind also affects the roll of the ball.

Set yourself realistic goals – occasionally a long putt drops but you should never be disappointed to get down in 2 strokes.

ROUGH STUFF

1 FIRM GRIP
The rough on the sandy dunes of a links is left largely untouched. You often find yourself in dense, wiry grass. Reach for a lofted club and choose a direct route to safety. Grip tightly and stand open.

2 STEEP BACKSWING
Pick the club up sharply on the backswing, breaking the wrists early. A steep backswing is essential because it helps you swing the club down into the ball. Aim to strike down on a patch of grass just behind the ball.

3 SAFELY OUT
Swing down steeply as hard as you can without losing control. Cut through as much grass around the ball as possible – this is no time for delicacy. The shot is tough on wrists so keep a firm grip on the club.

DEEP TROUBLE

Bunkers are hard to spot in the humps and hollows of a links course and devilishly difficult to escape from. A yardage chart comes in useful if you're not familiar with the course – it can perform the role of an experienced caddie.

Study the chart and lay up short of bunkers if necessary. Don't take risks – it's fine to sacrifice distance, particularly if it keeps you on the fairway.

When you land in a fairway pot bunker it's unlikely you have a direct route to the green – concentrate on making sure your next shot isn't from the same spot. The powdery fine sand is perfect for the high splash shot. Open your stance and keep the clubface open. Swing long and smooth on an out-to-in path.

Huge sandy dunes are punishing hazards that surround many fairways and greens. You're bound to be faced with an awkward stance and the thick, wiry grass doesn't let go of your ball easily.

Play your recovery with a sand wedge and grip the club tight. It's difficult to achieve any distance, so don't be too ambitious with your escape.

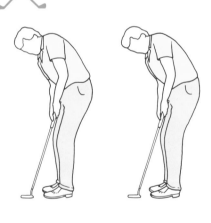

Run of the green
In a strong wind adopt a wider putting stance to give you more stability – it's extremely distracting to feel the wind buffeting you when you're trying to hole a putt.

Wind has a minimal effect on the line of short putts – but the run of your ball on a long putt is greatly affected by strong winds.

When you study the line of a long putt, take note of the wind direction as well as the slope on the green.

A ball stroked towards the hole in calm conditions leaves you with a simple tap in. But if you hit an identical putt into the wind, the ball pulls up well short. A crosswind sends the putt off line. It can also exaggerate the break on a putt – or cause the ball to run on a straighter line than it would in calm conditions.

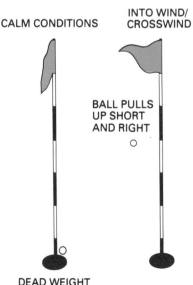

CALM CONDITIONS

INTO WIND/
CROSSWIND

BALL PULLS
UP SHORT
AND RIGHT

DEAD WEIGHT

Playing a US type course

Often superbly landscaped and impeccably maintained, US style courses are a delight to behold – but take care: their charms conceal some wicked ways. Plenty of water, rolling fairways, huge bunkers and slick running greens make the courses tough, but with the right technique they offer a fair test to your golf.

Ask any golfer to picture a US course and Augusta National, home of the US Masters, usually springs to mind. One of the best known in the world, this dream course is typical of American design. But you needn't be in the USA to have the opportunity of playing one of these magnificent monsters. This type of course architecture is becoming popular all over the world.

Water hazards are a prominent feature of US style courses and help to create some fearsome penal holes. Often there can be as much water as dry land – a snaking fairway or sculptured green provide the only safe haven. If your judgement and technique are sound, you can accurately predict how the ball behaves on landing. But you're never more severely punished for a mistake than you are on a water hole.

TROUBLED WATERS

While you have the luxury of a bridge over the water, your ball must take an aerial route. But it's not just the physical presence of water that has an effect on your golf – it's the psychological factor

▼ **DREAM COURSE**
US style courses are a dream to play, with impressive views at every turn. Dramatic water hazards, usually manmade, test your nerve and skill to the full. It's essential you adopt a positive mental attitude if you are to stay out of trouble. Seldom are you confronted by blind shots into greens – but water is everywhere, and shallow, sculptured bunkers are cleverly placed to gather your ball if a shot strays off line.

Unlike the traditional links course, the US style owes little to its natural setting. Artificial slopes are thrown up by massive earthmoving operations, and dense plantings of trees and shrubs overhang lakes and rolling fairways to form a perfectly manicured golf landscape.

as well.

Once you know the distance of the shot, have confidence in your club selection. If the green is very close to the water's edge, take one more club to allow for a slight miss-hit. Concentrate on making a smooth swing – just because there is water ahead, you don't have to hit the ball hard.

FINDING THE FAIRWAY

Plentiful supplies of water help keep the undulating fairways green all year round. Take a good look at the roll of each fairway before you tee off – aiming down the middle is not always the best option. Even a gentle slope may kick your ball off line, so predict the path of your

▼ MENTAL BLOCK
Faced with a shot over water the mind can often become awash with negative thoughts. The water looms large and the target almost fades into the background. This mental block is the making of a bad shot – it's usually followed by the depressing sight of ripples as your ball descends into a watery grave.

▼ **OPEN MIND**
The same hole without the hazards paints an entirely different picture. This is what you should visualize as you approach your ball. Block out the water from your mind as though it doesn't exist. Concentrate on your technique and play a positive shot to the green – confidence helps form a good swing.

shot along the ground as well as in the air.

If you're confident of reaching the green in regulation, look ahead and judge which is the best line into the flag. Concentrate on intelligent placement off the tee to blot out hazards from your mind and make ticklish approach shots less dangerous.

Because the grass is quite lush the ball often stops on slopes on the fairways. Remember, when the ball lies below your feet it has a tendency to fly to the right – align slightly left of target to compensate. With the ball above your feet it's easy to pull the shot to the left, so make sure you adjust your alignment accordingly.

The rough lining the fairways is always well defined and perfectly manicured. But it's often quite dense which makes it hard to judge how far the ball flies. Your control is reduced and a fade or draw is difficult to achieve. Weigh up your shot carefully and avoid ambitious carries – even the slightest miss-hit may end in disaster.

HAZARD PLAY

Large fairway bunkers are common on US type courses. Often a daunting sight from the tee, the bunkers are less punishing than they look. The traps are usually shallow and offer an escape route – and from a reasonable lie distance is seldom a problem.

Take one or two clubs more than you would from the same range on the fairway. Position the ball in the middle of your stance and grip down the club. Make a three-quarter backswing to give you maximum control and reduce the risk of hitting sand before the ball.

SLIPPERY SLOPES

This style of green is invariably quick and some of the slopes and undulations may be quite severe. Like every part of the course, the greens are heavily watered and ideal for target golf.

They look inviting and attractive to the eye, but if your approach shot lacks accuracy you are often faced with a treacherous chip or putt.

You must think of the pin position before you decide where to hit your ball. On receptive greens a high shot lands softly, so pitch the ball all the way to the flag and you can be confident of it stopping quickly.

Always aim to leave your ball below the hole – a 20ft (6.5m) putt uphill is far easier than half that distance down a slippery slope. Use this tactic with your approach shot, too. If you miss a green it's better to stray on the low side of the hole to give you a more straightforward chip back up the slope

to the pin.

American style greens are so fast and contoured it can often feel as if you're putting across a tilted table top. A long putt downhill requires a gentle touch and you may want to lag some putts rather than attack the hole.

The slopes of the green, variety of grass and direction of cut all determine the grain of the putting surface. Look closely at the grain and judge the likely effect on the roll of your ball.

When you're putting *with* the grain (grass growing away from you) the green appears light in colour and the putt is faster. The reverse is true when you putt *into* the grain (grass growing towards you) – the green looks relatively dark and the putt meets more resistance and is slower.

Read the break of the putt and picture the ball dying towards the hole. Don't be too aggressive or you risk racing the ball past. Always be grateful for two putting from long range.

pro tip

Practice opportunities
A great benefit of the US style of golf course design is the emphasis on practice facilities. Whenever you visit a course with a good practice ground, take a lead from the professionals and warm up before your round.

It's the perfect opportunity to check the basic fundamentals such as set-up and alignment. You also loosen up your golfing muscles and avoid the often destructive 1st tee stiffness.

Sight and sand
Greenside bunkers are often regarded with dread by the average golfer. But they can have a positive side – when several are knitted together on a hole they accentuate the shape and contours of the green. When you're some distance from the flag, this visual aid helps you place your approach shot.

Jack Nicklaus finds bunker clusters a great help, and uses them to good effect in his own designs. The course at St Mellion in Cornwall is a fine example, with bunkers hugging many of the greens. While it's hard to appreciate if your ball lands in one, intelligently placed bunkers are an integral and attractive feature of a hole.

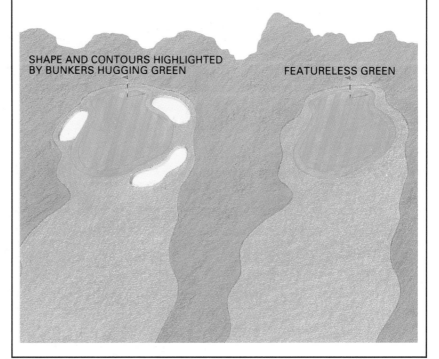

SHAPE AND CONTOURS HIGHLIGHTED BY BUNKERS HUGGING GREEN

FEATURELESS GREEN

Types of play

Golf involves a greater variety of competition than any other sport. You can tread the fairways on a wide range of courses and there are several types of game you can try.

Those who only play one form of golf week after week deny themselves the change of pace and strategy offered by other forms of competition. Each game produces excitement and a whole new range of challenges.

Probably the game most played around British courses at the weekend is **fourball best ball**. Usually arranged between groups of friends, this is one of the most enjoyable forms of matchplay.

It often produces quality golf because your partner is usually there to help out should you find trouble. This relieves pressure and encourages you to play more attacking golf.

Foursomes is the closest golf comes to becoming a team game. Partners share the same golf ball

MULTIPLE CHOICE
Most types of play appeal to every golfer – there's certainly plenty to choose from. Being aware of every one helps make your time on the course more enjoyable. Variety is also extremely good for your game – a head to head singles match provides the perfect opportunity to sharpen your competitive edge.

TYPES OF PLAY

FORMAT	RULES AND CONDITIONS
 **MATCHPLAY SINGLES**	Doing enough to beat your opponent is all that matters in matchplay. Many titles have been won with scores that would look quite ordinary in a strokeplay competition. Three-quarters of the difference in handicaps determines the number of strokes given or received over 18 holes. For example, if you have a handicap of 10 and your opponent plays off 19 you give 7 strokes (three-quarters of the 9 stroke difference = 6.75). Your opponent receives a shot on the holes where the stroke index is 7 or less. The winner is the golfer who manages to be up by more holes than there are left to play. For example the term 4 and 3 describes a victory where a player is 4 holes up on an opponent with only 3 holes to play – winning the remaining 3 holes is still not enough to get back on level terms. When you're dormie up on an opponent you're ahead by as many holes as there are to play – 3 up with 3 to play for instance. If a match is all square after 18, the winner is decided by playing extra holes. If a player wins on the first extra hole, it's described as a victory on the 19th.
 **STROKEPLAY**	In a medal strokeplay event you compete with the best golfers in the club on an even footing, because all players receive their full handicap allowance. Usually played in threes, the person with the lowest net score (number of shots less handicap) wins the competition. In the event of a tie, a system known as a countback usually decides the outcome. The score for the back nine holes on each card is taken and half the relevant handicap deducted to arrive at the lowest score. If this fails to break the deadlock, the back six holes are looked at with a third of each handicap deducted. This process continues – right down to the last hole if necessary – until a winner is found. Play-offs in strokeplay events are not unheard of, but because it's hard to arrange a mutually suitable date, they're far less common than countbacks.
 **FOURSOMES**	In this format you and your partner share the same ball and play alternate strokes. It's officially matchplay, but this form of golf can also be used for stableford and strokeplay events. Each partnership decides in advance who tees off on the even holes and who tees off on the odds. You keep to this format no matter who knocks in the putt on any given hole. To work out the number of strokes you give or receive in a matchplay competition, add together the handicaps of the two pairs and take three-eighths of the difference. Seldom do a great deal of shots change hands in a game of foursomes. In strokeplay foursomes the pair add together their handicaps and divide the total by two – this figure is then deducted from the final gross score.
FOURBALL BEST BALL	This form of golf is played in pairs with each golfer playing his own ball. The lowest score recorded by a pair on each hole is the one that counts. Strokes given or received in a matchplay competition are worked out as three-quarters of the difference in handicaps. The golfer with the lowest handicap gives strokes to the other three members of the fourball. In a strokeplay competition players receive three-quarters of their individual handicap. For example, if you play off 18 you receive 13.5 shots – this is rounded up to 14. So, on the holes where the stroke index is 14 or less the course effectively gives you a stroke. The fairest way to decide on partners in a fourball best ball is to throw up four golf balls – one belonging to each member of the group. The two balls which come down closest together determine who plays with who. This helps ensure there's a fair mix of handicaps. It also means you're not partnered with the same golfer every time.

FORMAT	RULES AND CONDITIONS
 **GREENSOMES**	There's one big difference between this game and foursomes. With greensomes every player tees off and each pairing decides which of their two drives is in the best position. Then the pair take alternate shots until the hole is completed. The handicap system for this form of play is the most complicated in golf, so it's a good idea to calculate it before you reach the 1st tee. The player with the lowest handicap in a pairing takes three-fifths of his handicap and the higher handicap player two-fifths of his handicap. The two figures are added together to arrive at the allowance for that pair in a strokeplay event. For example: Player A with a handicap of 12: three-fifths of 12 equals 7.2. Player B with a handicap of 16: two-fifths of 16 equals 6.4. Added together the strokes received equal 13.6 – this is rounded up to 14. In matchplay greensomes the calculation of handicaps is the same as for strokeplay. Three-quarters of the difference between the two pairs' total handicaps determines the number of shots given or received.
 **MIXED FOURSOMES**	Mixed foursomes are a familiar sight on most courses. This form of golf is identical to normal foursomes except for one important difference – each pairing consists of a male and female. The handicap allowances and rules of play don't differ in any way. It often gives the gents an opportunity to play longer shots into greens – and the ladies shorter ones – than they're used to.
 **JUNIOR SENIOR**	Most clubs organize challenge matches between teams of junior and adult golfers. As many clubs impose restrictions on the times young members may play, it gives juniors a rare opportunity to match their skills with the older members. Often a very competitive day, the format is usually matchplay singles, with the occasional fourball best ball. There are no allowances for age – handicaps are all that matter. Normal matchplay rules apply.
 **SINGLE PLAYER**	One of the great benefits of golf is that you only need yourself and a set of clubs to make up a game. As a single player one of the best games you can play is a competition with the course. Basically it's a game of matchplay against an invisible opponent in the form of par. Give yourself three-quarters of your handicap to determine how many shots you receive. From there on it's the same as any other game of matchplay – though you can't give yourself putts! As a single player you have no standing on the course. As a matter of etiquette you have to wave through other groups when necessary.

and play alternate shots. There's a certain camaraderie in foursomes, because the end result depends as much on your partner's performance as yours.

Greensomes is closely related to foursomes. This form of golf is very popular on society days and club invitation events – both of which usually involve 36 holes. Having had a refreshing lunch, it's a light - hearted and enjoyable way to spend the afternoon. The more serious competitions usually take place in the morning.

DREAM SCORES

Texas scramble is similar to an advanced form of greensomes. Partnerships can be made up of groups of two, three or four players.

Every player in the group tees off on every hole and they choose the best drive. From that spot each player hits a second shot. The partnerships then decide on the best position from which to play their third shots, and so on until one player holes out.

With each golfer having a go at every shot the handicap allowance is far from generous – one eighth of the combined handicaps being the number of strokes received.

Texas scramble is played in a strokeplay format. It gives club golfers an opportunity to record the sort of scores they often see on television, but only dream about achieving themselves.

PLAY YOUR OWN GAME

Most clubs organize competitions on a regular basis, particularly in summer. The most popular is **medal strokeplay** – you're on your own here, with no partner to blame or rely on. In many ways, success is that much more satisfying in a strokeplay event because you know it's all down to you.

The **stableford** system was invented in 1931 and is one of the more recent introductions to the selection of golf games. You record points according to your score on each hole – one point for a bogey, two for a par, three for a birdie and so on.

You receive seven-eighths of your full handicap in a stableford competition. For example if you play off 16, the course gives you a shot on each of the holes with a

Mutual concession
In a friendly knock with nothing at stake there's no rule stating you have to hole out every putt. Many golfers agree on the 1st tee that a ball coming to rest inside the grip of your putter is conceded.

This is ideal if you're playing an evening game and the light is fading fast. It's also a good idea when the greens are in poor condition and you want to preserve your silky smooth putting stroke.

However, before you agree to this change in the rules, make sure your opponent doesn't have a broom handle putter similar to the one used by Sam Torrance!

stroke index of 14 or less – shoot par on one of these holes and you notch up three points for a net birdie.

A high handicap golfer may receive more than one stroke on some of the harder holes on the course. If you're a low handicapper and this makes you feel a little hard done by, think again – golfers with handicaps better than scratch find themselves in the unenviable situation of giving strokes to the course. To them a birdie may be worth only two points.

The beauty of the stableford format is that you can have a complete disaster on one hole and still not ruin your chances of winning. If you drop two shots on a hole or comfortably run into double figures, the result is the same – zero points for that hole.

Singles matchplay is competitive head to head stuff. As with all matchplay games you may not have to hole out every time – short putts can be conceded. However, don't be too quick to give your opponent a short putt early in the

round – on the 1st green they're easily missed.

Eclectic competitions are run over a pre-determined number of rounds and require several strokeplay cards to be returned. At the end of the allotted period the cards for each competitor are sorted. The lowest score returned for each of the 18 holes is taken to arrive at the final total.

Over a period of years it can be a great morale boost for the club golfer. Scores in the 40s are quite realistic – and for someone who seldom breaks 80 this can be a very comforting thought.

KEEP IT COMPETITIVE

As for gambling in private matches there's no one to tell you what stakes you should or shouldn't play for, except perhaps your dependants.

As long as you're fully aware of the stakes, and you understand the rules of the game, you have the recipe for enjoying every one of the many forms of golf.

Using your course planner

sed on the professional tour for decades, course planners – also known as yardage charts – are quite a recent introduction to the amateur game. They started to become popular with club players in the early '80s.

There's little doubt that a yardage chart can prove useful, particularly when you're on a strange course. It tells you the exact distance to the flag – wherever you are – and also helps you steer clear of any trouble that might be waiting for you along the way.

However, there are several points you need to bear in mind if you intend making the most of the information contained in your course planner. If you don't fully understand a yardage chart it can be a totally useless pocket filler – it may even land you in more trouble than you deserve.

TEE TO GREEN

Distances to each green are marked in black on most charts. Your first job should be to check whether they are measured to the front or to the centre of the green. You can usually find this information on the inside front cover of the booklet.

You must be clear on this point –

there's almost no end to the number of disasters that might befall you if you get it wrong.

The figures printed in red describe distances from the tee. Bear in mind that there is more than one teeing area on almost every course – there can be up to three or four on some championship venues.

This means you may have to work out a few sums in your head before you decide on a club to use. Make a note of the tee you're playing from and take into account the difference in yardages. A bunker that's out of reach from the back marker may gladly welcome your

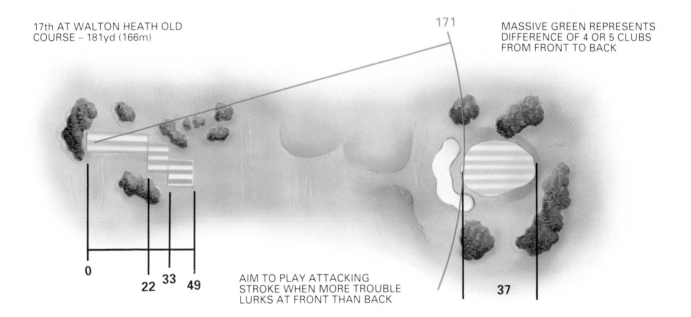

17th AT WALTON HEATH OLD COURSE – 181yd (166m)

171

MASSIVE GREEN REPRESENTS DIFFERENCE OF 4 OR 5 CLUBS FROM FRONT TO BACK

0

22 33 49

AIM TO PLAY ATTACKING STROKE WHEN MORE TROUBLE LURKS AT FRONT THAN BACK

37

BETTER SAFE THAN SORRY
Many golfers fail to make the most of course planners when they tee up on par 3s. The numbers on the tee marker tell you how far it is to the centre of the green, but you need to take other important factors into account.

The 17th on the Old Course at Walton Heath is a good example. On a huge green like this it's not enough simply to know the distance to the centre of the green. You need to be aware of exactly how far it is to the flag if you're to hit your ball close. The putting surface spans the best part of 40yd (36m) from front to

back. This probably represents a difference of as much as three or four clubs, so a careless choice here can leave you with a monster of a putt.

Your main priority is to clear the bunker that eats into the front of the green – leaving your ball short is almost unforgivable when there's more trouble at the front than there is at the back. Use your course planner to make sure you give yourself some margin for error – with this much green to work with, only your worst duff should land in the bunker. There may be holes on your home course where you can apply this theory too – you don't have to be at Walton Heath.

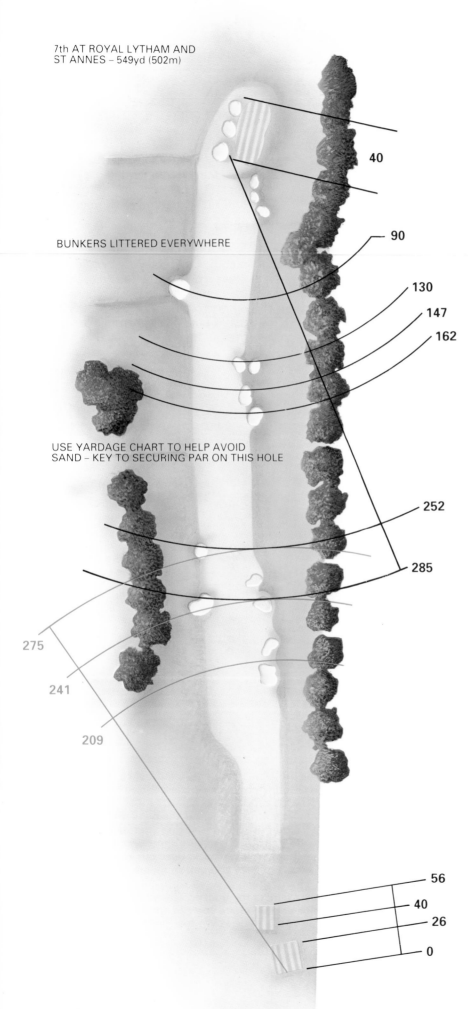

7th AT ROYAL LYTHAM AND
ST ANNES – 549yd (502m)

BUNKERS LITTERED EVERYWHERE

USE YARDAGE CHART TO HELP AVOID
SAND – KEY TO SECURING PAR ON THIS HOLE

40

90

130

147

162

252

285

275

241

209

56

40

26

0

PATH FINDER
The 7th at Royal Lytham and St Anne's is a real monster of a hole – 549yd (502m), well out of reach in 2, and littered with bunkers, ditches and gorse bushes. A sensible frame of mind is the key to securing your par on holes as long as this. A go for broke attitude is unlikely to do wonders for your score.

Make your passage down this fairway as smooth and as easy as possible. This means identifying hazards, finding out how far they are from your ball, and then selecting the club that enables you to give them a wide berth. This is where your yardage chart comes in.

A group of bunkers comes into play around the 200yd (180m) mark, so the first job is to stay out of the sand with your drive. Don't be afraid to take a lofted wood off the tee to achieve this – even on a long hole. If it means your next shot can be played from a good lie on the fairway, you've made the right decision.

The next stage is to give yourself the best possible chance of hitting the green with your third shot – once again this means finding a position on the fairway and not in the sand.

All the way along this hole your overall strategy should be position, not power. Remember, the less pressure you put on yourself in a round of golf the better – use the course planner to help you achieve just that.

ball from the front tee. Equally, you may be able to carry hazards you wouldn't dream of firing over from the back tee.

GREEN CARD

The length of a green is often neglected when looking at a course planner. However, it's a valuable nugget of information – particularly on a flat hole where it's difficult to grasp the overall perspective, or on a hole with a raised green where you can't see the putting surface.

From a long way out, greens tend to look shorter than they really are, so a yardage chart can help you judge how far on to the putting surface a hole is cut.

OVER THE HILL
The 3rd on the Kings Course at Gleneagles is a picturesque hole in keeping with the beautiful surroundings. It's not long either – only 374yd (342m). But nothing can hide the degree of difficulty on this unique hole.

The drive isn't a problem. A lone bunker lurks on the left of the fairway – while it's around the distance you hit your tee shot, you should still be able to avoid it without too much trouble.

It's when you approach the second shot that your yardage chart comes in very handy. The hump in the middle of the fairway could almost be a mountain – the flag would need to be at least 50ft (15m) high for you to see it from the level of the fairway. It's as blind a shot as you could ever imagine on a golf course.

There's nothing to stop you wandering up to take a look at the green, but because you're at such a high level, judging distance is extremely difficult. Your eyes tell you what lies in wait over the hill, but you need your course planner to gauge the exact distance to the flag. This is the main problem on blind holes – the severity of some slopes upsets your ability to judge distance accurately. In these situations more than any other a yardage chart justifies the money you spend on it.

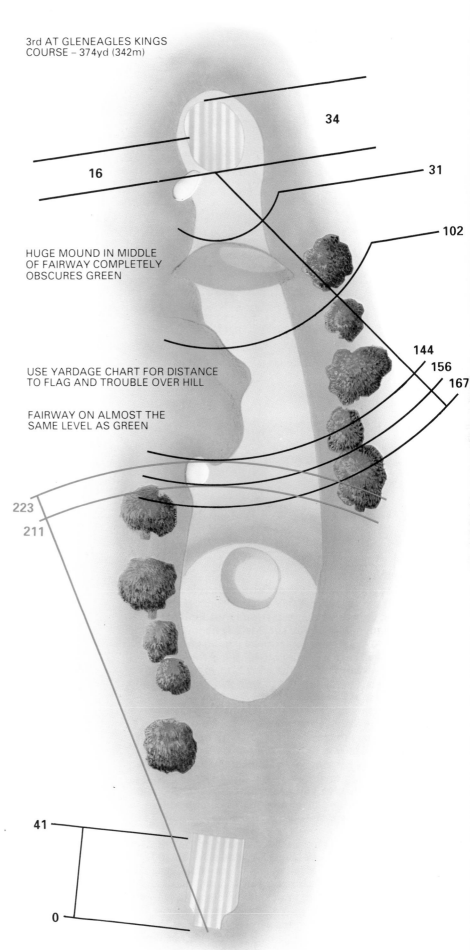

3rd AT GLENEAGLES KINGS COURSE – 374yd (342m)

34

16

31

102

HUGE MOUND IN MIDDLE OF FAIRWAY COMPLETELY OBSCURES GREEN

144

156

167

USE YARDAGE CHART FOR DISTANCE TO FLAG AND TROUBLE OVER HILL

FAIRWAY ON ALMOST THE SAME LEVEL AS GREEN

223

211

41

0

While yardage charts have a valuable role to play in negotiating your way round a course, you must not become totally dependent on them. Your eyes are an equally integral part of the process, giving you information in three dimensions, not just two.

EXTRA PAIR OF EYES

However, one task the human eye cannot perform is detecting hidden danger. On undulating ground it's easy for ditches and bunkers to be all but invisible from the tee. A quick glance at the yardage chart can help you pick your way through unknown territory. This is perhaps the most valuable function a course planner can perform.

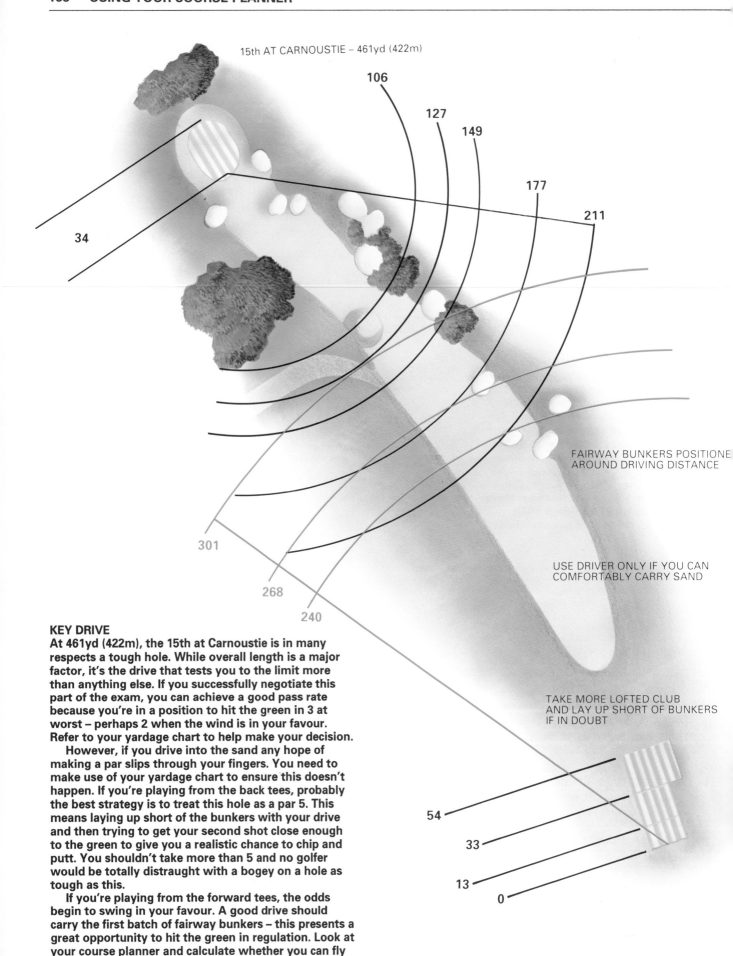

15th AT CARNOUSTIE – 461yd (422m)

106
127
149
177
211
34
301
268
240

FAIRWAY BUNKERS POSITIONE
AROUND DRIVING DISTANCE

USE DRIVER ONLY IF YOU CAN
COMFORTABLY CARRY SAND

TAKE MORE LOFTED CLUB
AND LAY UP SHORT OF BUNKERS
IF IN DOUBT

54
33
13
0

KEY DRIVE

At 461yd (422m), the 15th at Carnoustie is in many respects a tough hole. While overall length is a major factor, it's the drive that tests you to the limit more than anything else. If you successfully negotiate this part of the exam, you can achieve a good pass rate because you're in a position to hit the green in 3 at worst – perhaps 2 when the wind is in your favour. Refer to your yardage chart to help make your decision.

However, if you drive into the sand any hope of making a par slips through your fingers. You need to make use of your yardage chart to ensure this doesn't happen. If you're playing from the back tees, probably the best strategy is to treat this hole as a par 5. This means laying up short of the bunkers with your drive and then trying to get your second shot close enough to the green to give you a realistic chance to chip and putt. You shouldn't take more than 5 and no golfer would be totally distraught with a bogey on a hole as tough as this.

If you're playing from the forward tees, the odds begin to swing in your favour. A good drive should carry the first batch of fairway bunkers – this presents a great opportunity to hit the green in regulation. Look at your course planner and calculate whether you can fly the sand with your drive. You should be able to do this comfortably – if clearing the sand relies on you hitting your best ever drive, the gamble is probably not worth taking.

Raised and sunken greens

Many golfers are baffled by why they can't hit the ball close to the flag on elevated or sunken greens. Even though their striking and direction may be good the result can be disappointing because of poor club selection.

Understand the flight of the ball when hit up or downhill, and how the ball behaves when it pitches – these are the keys to playing to different green levels.

UPHILL STRUGGLE

When playing to a raised green a ball pitches on the putting surface before it can fly its full normal distance. To combat the effect of the slope you must play more club than the yardage suggests.

Too often you see players struggling to reach the green when firing uphill. They choose too little club and fall short of the target – the ball frequently rolls back down the slope.

The more elevated the green is, the more club you must hit. But however steep the slope you should never need to go up more than two clubs in calm conditions.

You must also take flight path into account. The ball comes in on a lower path than normal, and it runs on landing – more so as the green is likely to be well drained and firm.

UP AND DOWN DALE

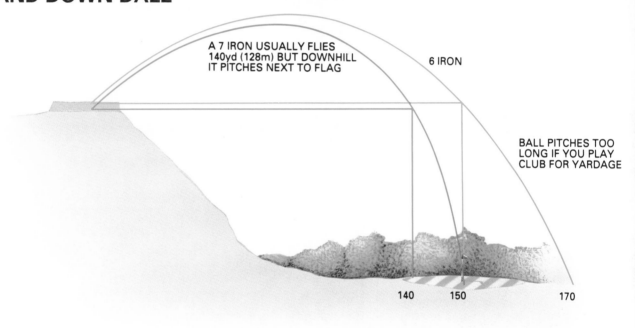

A 7 IRON USUALLY FLIES 140yd (128m) BUT DOWNHILL IT PITCHES NEXT TO FLAG

6 IRON

BALL PITCHES TOO LONG IF YOU PLAY CLUB FOR YARDAGE

140   150   170

▲ **When firing downhill to a sunken green, select one club less than the yardage suggests. The ball crosses a point level with the tee, then drops further until it pitches close to the flag. Even though you hit only one less club the distance between where the shots land is considerable.**

Choosing the club you normally hit for the distance lands you in trouble – the ball pitches beyond the green.

▼ **The opposite applies when shooting up to an elevated green. To play a shot to the target you must select a club that would pitch beyond the flag on level ground. If you rely on just the yardage and choose your usual club for the distance, the ball falls short.**

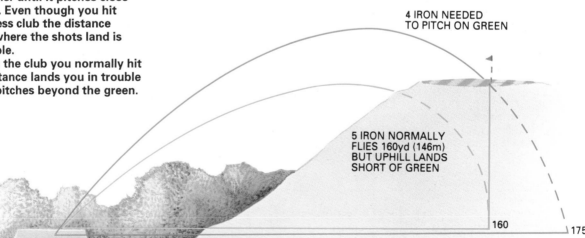

4 IRON NEEDED TO PITCH ON GREEN

5 IRON NORMALLY FLIES 160yd (146m) BUT UPHILL LANDS SHORT OF GREEN

160   175

Try to hit the shot slightly higher than usual to help you stop on the putting surface. Aim to pitch the ball on the green but short of the hole.

DOWNHILL DEADEYE

When played downhill to a green the ball is in the air longer than usual so it flies further. Play less club than the yardage suggests – hitting your usual club could mean the ball pitching in trouble over the back of the green. But beware of playing *too* little club as the ball may land on the downslope and shoot through the green and into trouble.

You can afford to be bold and pitch the ball right up to the flag. The shot stops quickly as sunken greens are usually softer than normal and the ball drops from a steep angle.

The most your clubbing should vary is by two on a still day. In a head or cross wind, take more club and play a three-quarter shot to keep the ball low – this gives you greater control.

SHORT AND RUNNING

If you are faced with a downhill shot which is also downwind you may find that you can't pitch the ball on the green without it bounding through the back, leaving you a tricky shot back.

Provided there is no trouble between you and the green and the ground is firm, it's best to play a shot that lands short and bounces on. But make sure you reach the green – or your next shot could be equally tricky.

pro tip

Down and upslope lies
When firing down to a sunken green you often have to play off a downhill lie. Position the ball slightly further back in your stance – lessening the chance of a thin – and flex your right knee more than usual to compensate for the slope. The ball flies low and from left to right, so choose your club, and aim, carefully.

On an upslope, push the ball forward in your stance, flex your left knee and remember the ball flies high and right to left.

masterclass

Langer's thoughtful clubbing
Bernhard Langer is one of the world's most accurate iron players. He knocks both long and short irons close to the flag with amazing regularity.

The sinewy German is also a great strategist and prepares for each stroke thoroughly. He fully understands how a ball behaves when going either up or downhill, and can choose a club which he knows should go close provided he hits it solidly and straight.

If the 134yd (123m) 2nd at Woburn was on the level instead of being set in a deep dell, Langer would probably hit an 8 iron. But because the hole is so far below his feet a pitching wedge is the sensible choice.

Even though Bernhard usually hits a 5 iron about 180yd (165m), he would choose more club to tackle the famous uphill 179yd (164m) 14th at Wentworth to combat the effect of the upslope. He relies on crowd reaction to tell him if the shot finishes close.

Langer tees off at Woburn's 2nd, with its sunken green.

Think like a pro

You can shave vital strokes off your score by taking a sensible and calculated approach to every shot you play. Thinking strategically is just as important as confidence. All top professionals carefully weigh up each shot to decide which option is the best for the situation.

KNOW YOUR LIMITS

It's vital to know the distance you hit each club for any strategies to work. A yardage chart is extremely helpful when used in the right way, but is useless if you don't know how far you hit the ball.

Most club players use a chart only for their second shots – if at all – but pros consult it on the tee. They look at what trouble there is and how far off the tee it is. They don't automatically take a driver at a reachable par 5 hole when they know that some cross bunkers are in range. A long iron is shorter and safe but still means they can reach the green in 2.

Use yardages in a positive way.

THOUGHT PROCESS

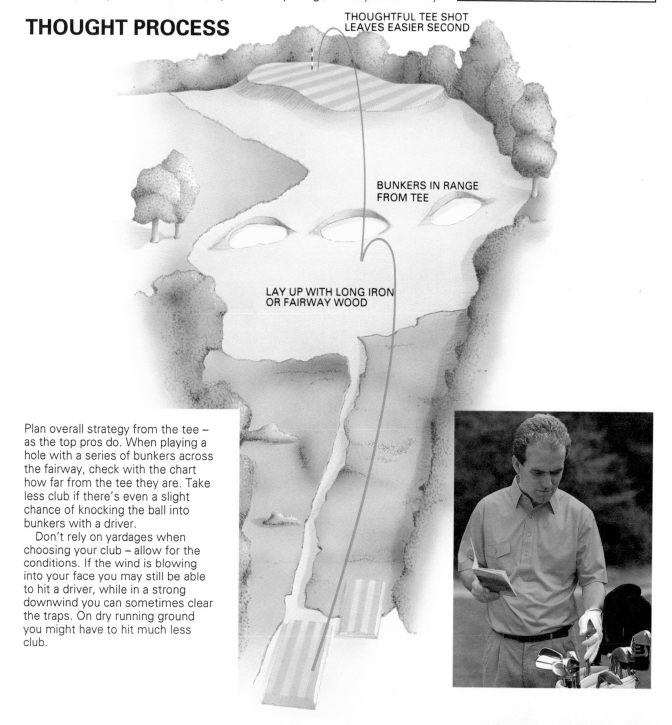

THOUGHTFUL TEE SHOT LEAVES EASIER SECOND

BUNKERS IN RANGE FROM TEE

LAY UP WITH LONG IRON OR FAIRWAY WOOD

Plan overall strategy from the tee – as the top pros do. When playing a hole with a series of bunkers across the fairway, check with the chart how far from the tee they are. Take less club if there's even a slight chance of knocking the ball into bunkers with a driver.

Don't rely on yardages when choosing your club – allow for the conditions. If the wind is blowing into your face you may still be able to hit a driver, while in a strong downwind you can sometimes clear the traps. On dry running ground you might have to hit much less club.

Check the carry you need to clear bunkers at the corner of a dog-leg. Judge the wind and see if you can carry the trap with a driver. You may be able to make the hole a lot shorter. But never try to shorten the hole if the trouble around is too severe. A pro is content to take an iron to the corner of the dog-leg to be safe.

TWO SHOTS AHEAD

Being clever with your placement from the tee is an asset to your game. You should always think two shots ahead when deciding what club to play and where to aim. Unless a short par 4 is drive-able, it's often wise to hit a long iron from the tee to leave yourself a full shot in with a wedge. A driver can leave you an awkward length pitch that's difficult to judge – a full wedge is easier to control.

When possible look at the green in the distance and try to see which side the flag is on. If the hole is cut behind a bunker on the left try to fire your tee shot down the right to leave yourself an easier approach shot.

Always assess the profile of the hole. Most pros shape the ball from the tee away from trouble, or along the contours of the hole – a ploy you should try to copy.

With bunkers down the left it's best to fade the ball away from them. Aim slightly inside the bunkers and hit the ball left to right. Even if you hit the ball straight you shouldn't land in sand. On a sweeping dog-leg right hit a draw to hug the contours of the fairway.

The shape of the hole also dictates which side of the tee you should play from. Don't just play from the middle of the tee – you can make your second shot easier by teeing up in the right place. You should play from the left side of the tee on a dog-leg right.

GATHER KNOWLEDGE

Don't think ahead just from the tee – approach shots need mapping out too. If a green is sloping you must aim to the high side so that the ball runs round to the flag. On a very steeply sloping green, choose a club that keeps the ball below the hole for easier uphill putting.

Every time you go out on to a course you should try to learn the subtleties of each hole. Look to see where the trouble is and how the green slopes, and work out the best way to play the hole for future reference. Gather as much information as possible, and in all types of weather – strategies must change to suit the conditions if they're to pay off.

Concentrate hard and use this knowledge to work your way down the holes. Take your time to assess the situation on every shot you play. Never rush – but don't dwell on the shot. Once you have made up your mind what's needed play promptly. Try not to think of the trouble – top pros nurture only positive thoughts.

Shot preparation

Playing golf well has a lot to do with how you approach each shot. Choosing the right club and imagining the shape of shot is critical. You should take into account the weather, character of hole, ground conditions and the yardage.

The top pros – such as Colin Montgomerie – use their caddies to give an accurate yardage and also to help them work out what type of shot is needed to get a good result. Work together with a friend on a practice round. Always prepare thoroughly but be quick – never stew over the stroke.

masterclass

Faldo's game plan

Nick Faldo is the master strategist. He has total confidence in his game and never asks too much of himself. At the 1990 US Open he needed a birdie at the 72nd to go into the play-off. Though the hole was a long tricky par 4, Faldo still hit an iron off the tee. To stand any chance of achieving the 3 he needed he had to hit the fairway, as the rough was thick.

A driver was risky even though he would have had a shorter second shot, so he was content to hit an iron and then a 3 iron into the green. Nick's approach ended up 15ft (5m) away so his strategy paid off – but sadly his putt just missed.

Dog-leg strategy

Golf courses would be very dull if all the holes were straight. A major part of a player's enjoyment is to be able to manoeuvre the ball down and around varying shapes of hole using their skill and judgment. Tricky dog-legs are the ultimate challenge for the strategist.

Never take on a dog-leg hole before you have worked out exactly how you should play it. Look to see what you can gain by playing a particular shot off the tee – perhaps a draw to shape the

TIGHT AND TRAUMATIC
The 18th at Valderrama in Spain is a classic finishing hole. It severely tests your drive and approach, and to play it well both must be spot on. The hole is tight and unless your drive finds the fairway at the corner of the dog-leg, you're blocked out from the green by trees.

There are two strategies you can use to tackle this corking right-to-left hole. One is to calculate the distance to the corner – 220yd (200m) from the yellow tees – and settle for a positional shot with a touch of draw to leave a clear view

of the green. The other is a brave drive with draw down the edge of the trees on the left that bounds around the corner. This leaves a much shorter approach to the green.

But there is no need to be frightened by it or any other dog-leg holes – they needn't be a traumatic experience if your strategy and striking are good. Concentrate on the basics of the set-up and swing, and choose your club and type of shot wisely, to conquer even the trickiest of dog-legs.

417m (456yd) 18th VALDERRAMA

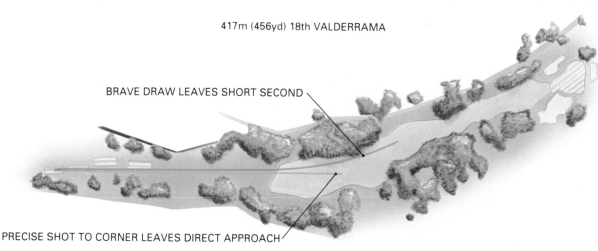

BRAVE DRAW LEAVES SHORT SECOND

PRECISE SHOT TO CORNER LEAVES DIRECT APPROACH

TEMPTING CARRY

Often a dog-leg hole presents you with an inviting challenge – an opportunity to cut the corner. In the right conditions the 18th on the Duke's course at Woburn (the 17th for a championship) is driveable for long hitters by carrying the tall trees on the right. Though the hole is listed at 356yd (325m) from the back, the tee is brought forward slightly for a tournament to tempt the pros to go for it.

This strategy of hitting over the corner instead of laying up with an iron can be a match winner. But never let your heart rule your head and attempt something out of your scope – there are only a few times when you should go for it.

Whenever you have a chance of taking on a big carry over a corner, you must weigh up the situation. Ask yourself what you gain. It may be that the risks outweigh the advantages and you should settle for the sensible lay-up.

356yd (325m) 18th WOBURN DUKE'S COURSE

SAFE LAY UP WITH IRON

BIG CARRY CUTS OFF CORNER

DRIVING DOWN THE BURMA ROAD

441yd (403m) 13th WENTWORTH WEST COURSE

DRIVE UP RIGHT - CLEAR APPROACH

The West Course at Wentworth – nicknamed the Burma Road – is littered with classic dog-legs each needing a separate plan to negotiate it successfully.

At the 441yd (403m) 13th, placement is the key. If you're to have a straight shot into the green you must hit your drive down the right side of the fairway. Going too far left means you're blocked out from firing straight at the flag by trees. Even if you hit the left side of the fairway you still have to draw the ball to hit the green.

On every dog-leg try to assess where the green is and decide whether it's best to favour one side of the fairway. Life is made much simpler when you can hit direct approaches.

SHOT DOWN LEFT - BLOCKED OUT FROM GREEN

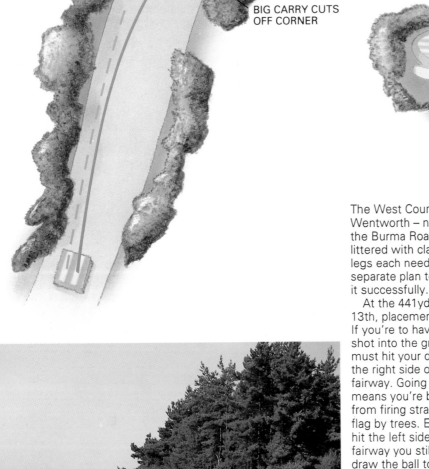

SHAPE YOUR COURSE

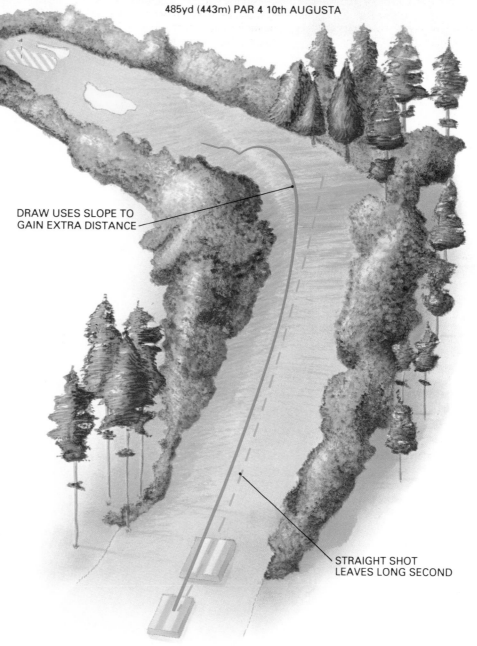

485yd (443m) PAR 4 10th AUGUSTA

DRAW USES SLOPE TO GAIN EXTRA DISTANCE

STRAIGHT SHOT LEAVES LONG SECOND

Most handicap players are content to hit the ball straight on every hole, but you should learn a lesson from the masters of golf. Shaping the ball – either a draw or fade – can be very advantageous at times. The 485yd (443m) Par 4 10th at Augusta is a sweeping right-to-lefter and the pros always look to hit a draw.

Steep slopes at the corner of the dog-leg can be used to their advantage. They can gain extra yardage by hitting a draw – as the slope takes the ball away closer to the hole. If you hit the ball straight, you risk staying up on the plateau. This leaves you over 215yd (195m) to the flag.

A draw that bounds down the slope can cut the yardage by over 30yd (27m). Instead of a 3 or 4 iron you can hit as little as a 6. This makes a real difference to your chances of making par.

Always look for an opportunity to use the contours of a hole to your advantage. Even if there are no slopes to use, a shaped drive is often the shot to keep the ball on the fairways.

ball round a long gradual right-to-left hole.

You may find that you need to hit an iron so you don't run out of fairway at the corner. Or you may have to play down one side or the other to leave yourself the best approach into the green. But what is certain is that no two dog-legs are exactly alike and need to be treated as individuals.

Weigh up all the dangers and check the yardages. One crucial yardage is the distance to the corner of the dog-leg if the angle is sharp, so you know what club to hit from the tee.

You may sometimes be tempted to cut the corner, so check how large the carry is. Be happy to play the percentage shot – don't attempt to clear a distance you know is on the edge of your limit.

CONTOUR HUGGING

Be prepared to shape your shots to gain an advantage. Often if you hit a straight shot – even on a gradual dog-leg – you can miss the fairway and find trouble. You may also leave yourself a longer next shot than if you shape the ball.

You can make a dog-leg easier just by standing in the proper place on the tee. When faced with a gradual left-to-right hole it's best to tee up on the left side of the hole. You don't have to shape the ball as much as you do from the right so it becomes a safer shot.

But if there is trouble down the right side – perhaps out of bounds – you should tee up on the right to play away from the danger.

masterclass

Woosnam's alternative way

The 18th at Augusta has ruined many players' dreams of pulling on the Master's green jacket. The 405yd (370m) hole dog-legs right, and under pressure it can be hard to hit the fairway.

The perfect tee shot is a fade, but you run the risk of letting it go into the trees on the right – especially when the nerves are tingling. But the main danger is the two gaping bunkers on the left.

In the 1991 Masters Ian Woosnam showed how you can use your imagination to conquer certain dog-legs.

Tied with Tom Watson coming to the final hole, he knew that if he tried to hit a cultured fade around the corner he might have come unstuck. After watching his rival cut a 3 wood into the trees, Woosie decided attack was the answer.

He blasted a driver straight over the fairway traps – a carry of 275yd (251m) on to the member's practice ground, which left him only an 8 iron into the green. He had trusted his power and avoided trying to be too clever by playing the conventional way.

Ian played up to the green, two putted and par was enough to beat off the challenge of Watson and the clubhouse leader Olazabal. Imagination secured his victory.